SUCCESS IN THE YEAR OF THE TIGER

Chinese Zodiac Horoscope 2022

Linda Dearsley

BENNION
KEARNY

Published in 2021 by Bennion Kearny

ISBN: 978-1-910515-89-1

Linda Dearsley has asserted her right under the Copyright, Designs and Patents Act, 1988 to be identified as the author of this book.

Bennion Kearny does not have any control over, or any responsibility for, any author or third-party websites mentioned in or on this publication.

A CIP catalogue record for this book is available from the British Library.

TABLE OF CONTENTS

CHAPTER 1: SUCCESS IN THE YEAR OF THE TIGER

Stand well back.

Drum roll, please!

Make way for the grand entrance of the magnificent Black Tiger.

That's the Year of the Black Tiger, of course, which bounds into the world on the 1st of February 2022, and swaggers on through until the 21st of January 2023.

If you've been feeling a little lacklustre, a little jaded, as the old Year of the Ox (that was 2021) finally lumbers off the stage, this could be the most exciting news in months. As Ox years fade, life often feels a bit stagnant, a bit dull. All that dutiful plodding, making progress – but painfully slowly – drives some signs crazy.

Well, if it's action you've been longing for, you're in for a treat. The Tiger of 2022 charges into the world like Lewis Hamilton roaring out of the pits for his umpteenth Grand Prix. Tiger energy is strong, bold, and fast-moving.

Tiger wants to get things done, NOW! After a full year of mind-numbingly patient slog, the Tiger arrives like an ice-cold shower to wake us all up, and kick us into action. *2022 is the year* to throw off the gloom, come out from under the duvet, and start living life like a fearless striped carnivore!

If you've got plans, if you're looking for adventure, this is the year to get out there and make it happen, with Tiger energy powering you every step of the way.

So, What Just Happened?

Well, for a start, we've just lived through probably the biggest global upheaval since World War II – courtesy of the revolutionary Rat of 2020 – intent on tearing down existing structures in order to replace them with something new. Aided and abetted, 12 months later, by his quieter companion… the Ox of 2021.

No wonder we're glum.

Although, at first glance, the Rat and the Ox look like polar opposites, and you'd expect the years they rule to be completely different, in fact, these two end up working as a team. Rat years and Ox years tend to operate as a pair. Rat starts the tumultuous process of change, often in dramatic style, then hands over to placid Ox to calm things down, smooth things out, and complete the job in an orderly manner.

Ox years are about endurance and putting in the groundwork to create a solid base through discipline, attention to detail, and a steady, methodical pace. Admirable qualities, of course, but after a whole 12 months of teeth-grindingly slow progress, enough is enough!

So, now we can wave goodbye to the Dodgy Duo and welcome in a potent new energy, just fizzing with vigour.

Tiger to the Rescue

According to the Chinese, the Tiger is the King of beasts. The God Tsai Shen Yeh is usually pictured riding into the world on a black tiger bringing wealth and good fortune. So, Tiger years are regarded as fortunate – though unpredictable – and Black Tiger years are even more favoured by the God.

Traditionally, Tigers are also associated with justice, so a lot of wrongs are set to be righted in Tiger years, and the big cat is also believed to be the guardian and protector of children. To this day, Chinese toddlers often wear shoes and clothing decorated with images of tigers to keep them safe.

To a certain extent, Tiger's care also extends to the weak and vulnerable in general. So, anyone harming these innocents is likely to feel the wrath of the Tiger this year.

Above all, Tiger energy arrives to heal the spirit-sapping lethargy of the departing Ox year and replace it with exuberant, life-affirming action. Bold, decisive moves are favoured; dithering and delay get penalised.

But just one note of caution. Don't get too carried away. Another Chinese proverb warns: 'If you ride the Tiger, it's difficult to get off.'

In other words, tread carefully and make sure you can finish what you start!

The Awesome Power of Black Water

Oddly enough, anyone tempted to take particularly reckless risks in 2022 is more likely to get away with their audacity than with any other Tiger year. That's because, just like people, not all Tigers are the same – and the sleek Black Tiger is probably the most sympathetic and tolerant member of the Tiger family.

Like all the creatures of the Chinese zodiac – the Tiger comes in five different varieties, or breeds, you might say – each with their own unique way of expressing the distinctive Tiger character. There are Water Tigers, Wood Tigers, Fire Tigers, Earth Tigers, and Metal Tigers.

2022 is the Year of the Water Tiger, known as the Black Tiger because black – as well as deep blue – is the colour that represents the Water element in the Chinese Calendar.

The Black Water Tiger is probably less fearsome and more accommodating than his flaming cousin, the Fire Tiger, but that doesn't make him a purring pussycat. A raging torrent can be just as destructive as a forest blaze.

The power of the Black Water Tiger is awesome. Handle with care.

Tame the Tiger to Make Your Dreams Come True

So, what will the Year of the Black Tiger bring for you? We're all hoping for better times ahead but are you brave enough to ride the Tiger, plunge full-tilt into the action, and let the striped cat carry you to your dream future? Or will you hang back, find a hidey-hole in the jungle, and wait it out until the big beast has gone by?

According to Chinese astrology, *it's up to you*. No matter what your sign, you get to choose how you're going to respond to the Tiger year – and the choices you make will shape your destiny in 2022. Play it clever, and you can get the power of the Tiger working for you. Get it wrong, and that feline energy could bat you around and around in circles, like a cat toying with a mouse.

Yet, the secret to taming the Tiger is deceptively simple. Once you understand the nature of the beast, and how it interacts with your particular sign, the path becomes clear. As soon as you know what you're dealing with, you can formulate your cunning plan!

Events, Dear Boy, Events...

It's said a journalist once asked retired Prime Minister Harold Macmillan what circumstances could throw a government off course and into turmoil.

'Events, dear boy!' the old man replied. 'Events.'

By which he meant, of course, unforeseen events. Naturally, few of us can use a crystal ball, but it's interesting to note this was a British Prime Minister. A Chinese head of state might well have given a different answer.

Not that the Chinese politician would claim to foretell the future – it's just that he or she, with their instinctive understanding of Chinese astrology, would know what sort of events could be expected from any particular year, so they'd be less likely to be taken by surprise.

In the West, we tend to think of each new year as an unwritten book just waiting for events to catapult out of nowhere to fill the blank pages. It's only when the year ends that we can look back and tell what sort of year it turned out to be.

In Chinese astrology, it's just the opposite. No year in Chinese astrology *is ever an anonymous blank*. Each arrives bristling with its own unique animal 'personality' – fully formed and ready to rock. People know what sort of year it's going to be from day one.

They believe that as the New Year dawns, a totally different animal energy has been unleashed on the world – and by understanding the effect that energy will have, they can work out what to expect and how to benefit.

Circumstances that might have led to uproar in a dramatic Dragon year could slide past in a tranquil haze when laid-back Goat is in charge. Similarly, an experimental, don't-bother-with-dull-details approach might impress massively when inquisitive Monkey grabs the wheel, but attempt such sloppiness on Ox's watch, and you'll find yourself in deep trouble. It really pays to get to know the boss!

4

The Transforming Black Tiger

As the year begins, it's obvious there's a lot of lost momentum to make up, and the Tiger intends to hit the ground running. The strength of this new energy could be overwhelming for some. Projects that had to be abandoned or put on hold during the pandemic can now be resurrected, preferably – as far as Tiger's concerned – at lightning speed. The pace of the turnaround may come as a shock to some signs and leave them feeling vaguely disoriented, but there's no need to be too alarmed.

At heart, the Black Tiger is an *idealistic reformer*. He really does want to make the world a better place, and he's been waiting a long time to have a crack at the task.

It's been 60 years since the last Black Tiger padded sinuously out to greet the dawn. Over half a century of watching and waiting. So, to get an insight into what kind of developments Black Tiger might inspire, we can take a look at what happened when his grandpa – the Black Tiger of 1962 – took charge.

Introducing the Trendy Black Tiger of 1962

As daylight broke on the morning of February 5th, 1962, the previous Black Tiger to rule the year strolled out to survey a world that – in many ways – was very similar in mood to the one our latest Black Tiger inherits in 2022.

The revolutionary Metal Rat of 1960 had swept in like a hurricane, as Metal Rats do, ripping away the staid, old-fashioned world left behind after World War II and preparing the ground for what turned out to be the youth-quake that was the swinging 60s. His plodding partner, the conscientious Ox of 1961, then moved in to ensure the seeds of change were firmly planted, and by 1962 it was left to the Black Tiger to pick up the pieces and assemble them into a bold new future.

Sounds familiar? In 1962, just like now, a lot of people were left confused and dismayed by recent upheavals and unsure where it all might lead. Yet, as the invigorating energy of the Black Tiger started to spread, a robust, big-cat confidence began to build.

Trail-Blazers in the White House

In the USA, the new young President John F Kennedy was just getting into his stride. Kennedy was thrilled by the futuristic idea of space exploration. That year, astronaut John Glenn became the first American to orbit the Earth, and a jubilant Kennedy was inspired to repeat his crazy vow that the USA would put a man on the Moon before the decade was over.

Meanwhile, his wife, Jacqueline Kennedy, was carving out her own novel approach to the role of First Lady. On Valentine's Day, she amazed the world by inviting TV viewers to take a look at the renovations she'd been making to the White House. She not only threw open the doors, she conducted the public on a televised tour of the residence. The first time a president's wife had ever done such a thing. The documentary caused a sensation, and was watched by over 80 million people around the globe.

It also gave viewers a further chance to admire Jackie's taste in clothes as well as wallpaper. Soon the Jackie 'look' – figure-hugging dresses and skirt suits teamed with boxy jackets – was firmly entrenched and Mrs Kennedy had become a fashion icon as well as the President's wife. By 1962, the Kennedys were regarded as a golden couple. Charming photographs of their young children – Caroline, age five and John Junior, just two – playing hide and seek in the Oval Office delighted the public, and the White House became a byword for youthful glamour.

Suddenly, Other World Leaders Looked Old and Drab

In Britain, Harold Macmillan was still Prime Minister, but he'd been in power since 1957 and the charismatic Kennedys made the Mac government look elderly and out of touch. In an effort to keep up, Macmillan dismissed one-third of his cabinet overnight in the most brutal reshuffle in British political history. The incident became known as the Night of the Long Knives, and 'Supermac' was re-nicknamed 'Mac the Knife'. He replaced his ministers with younger men, but it didn't help. He was out of office the following year.

An Explosion of Creativity

Tigers are associated with the novel and the new, while the Water element enhances communication, so it's not surprising that 1962 saw a huge upsurge in the arts, particularly music. In the USA, a young folk singer named Bob Dylan, age 21, performed his new song *Blowin' in the Wind* at a club in Greenwich Village, New York. (Decades later, the song was to be named one of the greatest of all time.) He followed it up a few months later with *A Hard Rain's a-Gonna Fall*.

In Britain, a new band calling themselves The Rolling Stones launched at London's Marquee Club, while the Beatles had their first original hit with *Love Me Do*. They also welcomed Ringo Starr into the group.

There was even a mild scandal when the most glamorous star of the era, Marilyn Monroe, stood up at a birthday bash for JFK in Madison Square Garden to serenade him with a sexy rendition of 'Happy Birthday Mr President' while dressed in a gown so snug that it was described by one commentator as 'basically skin and beads'.

Since there were already rumours circulating that Monroe and Kennedy were having an affair, it's unlikely Mrs Kennedy enjoyed the performance.

And it wasn't just the Music Scene...

That year, the first James Bond film, *Dr No*, hit the screens, legendary ballerina Margot Fonteyn began her sensational dancing partnership with Rudolph Nureyev in a performance of *Giselle*, an unlikely new comedy *Steptoe and Son* (about a scruffy father and son's Rag-and-Bone business) delighted TV viewers in Britain, and a young artist named Andy Warhol launched his first pop art exhibition in LA with a perplexing collection that included a picture of Campbell's soup cans.

Meanwhile, the incredibly popular Ford Cortina took to the tarmac, and a strange new super-hero – Spiderman – appeared in Marvel Comics.

To speed it all along, the audio cassette was invented that year, and the communications satellite Telstar shot into space, beaming the first live TV pictures between the USA and Europe – an event so inspiring the British band The Tornadoes recorded an instrumental single of the same name which promptly went to number one, on both sides of the Atlantic.

Yet, A Tiger's Always a Tiger...

There's no doubt Tiger years bring many benefits, but it would be a mistake to forget that the Tiger, even the comparatively benevolent Black Water Tiger, is still a wild beast.

As a result, 1962 saw its share of unfortunate events. The impetus to travel and communicate associated with the Water element that sent men into space and inspired satellites to be launched can – under the influence of the Tiger – become too strong, leading to disaster. Although John Glenn returned safely from his space adventure and Telstar was a success, 1962 also saw around six major plane crashes, several involving Boeing 707s, and in most cases there were no survivors. Then, under the powerful Water element, there were floods in Germany and Spain in which hundreds of people died, and thousands lost their homes.

Meanwhile, 36-year-old Marilyn Monroe, who'd started the year so well, was suddenly found dead in August, apparently of an overdose, and in

South Africa, Nelson Mandela – who'd been making a name for himself as an anti-apartheid revolutionary – was imprisoned in what was to become a life sentence.

In the UK, just before Christmas, the infamous Big Freeze set in – heralding the coldest winter since 1740. Snow lay on the ground for an unprecedented 62 consecutive days. Milkmen were pictured doing their rounds on skis, a man cycled on the Thames near Windsor Bridge, and in many a sheltered coastal bay, the sea froze over. There was not a frost-free night until March 5th 1963.

Yet, of all these unsettling events, by far the most terrifying was the Cuban Missile Crisis in which a confrontation between the USA and Russia (after Russia was found to have built nuclear missile bases on Cuba – within striking distance of Florida just 90 miles away) almost led to nuclear war.

For several frightening days, the world held its breath, then both leaders backed down, the missiles were removed, and catastrophe was averted.

The Dawning of the Green Revolution

Amidst the fear and drama of the missile episode, with the very real prospect of World War III breaking out, it was understandable that perhaps what was to turn out to be the most far-reaching event of 1962 passed almost unnoticed. It was merely the publication of a book – a work called *Silent Spring* by Rachel Carson – but it was a book that was to go on to inspire the modern environmental movement.

At the time, Rachel Carson was a New York writer of natural history, and she'd become increasingly alarmed at the effect the newly-introduced pesticides, which were being used in ever-increasing quantities, were having on birds. She published her findings in the ground-breaking book *Silent Spring* and drew attention to the devastating consequences chemicals and pollution were having on wildlife. One day soon, she suggested, we'd wake up to a Spring without birdsong or buzzing bees. She described pesticides as 'elixirs of death'.

Rachel's book reverberated down the decades, arousing growing concern. It led eventually to the banning of DDT and a movement that continued to gain more and more momentum with every passing year.

Get Ready to Rock

If 2021 was the year of 'Keep Calm and Carry On', 2022 couldn't be more different. That kind of dreary, cautious approach doesn't appeal to the Tiger for a second, and it will be jettisoned immediately. 2022 is more the year of 'Not Putting Up With It A Moment Longer!' On

February 1st, it's as if a cosmic alarm clock goes off but at a pitch inaudible to the human ear. We won't hear it, but sensitive types might feel it as Tiger energy pours in.

Oddly enough, though the world is a very different place in the 21st century to the world the last Black Tiger roamed, there are striking similarities in mood.

In 1962, everyone was thrilled by the idea of space exploration, and great strides were made in the technology. Yet, somehow, in the intervening decades, interest waned. Not anymore. Today, space fever is back. Now we've got millionaires and billionaires vying with each other for places on rocket ships, and space tourism for all is no longer a fantasy but looks like becoming reality quite soon.

Excited yet Nervous

Yet alongside the optimism that inspires us to reach for the stars, there's a pervading sense of fear, particularly among the young. In 1962, it was the serious possibility of nuclear destruction that kept people awake at night and had them building bomb shelters in the back garden. Now their grandchildren are just as worked up about climate change.

Different cause but the same sense of impending doom.

Yet that's Tiger all over. Bold and optimistic, yet fiercely protective of the planet. On Tiger's watch, we won't be able to close our eyes to the damage being done. Protests over the destruction of the Earth will get bigger and more dramatic in 2022. Green politics will become more and more important, and politicians who try to ignore environmental issues are likely to find themselves abandoned.

Riding The Tiger

This is the year to launch a business, revive an abandoned project, or invent something – preferably something environmentally beneficial or likely to aid the needy. The wilder and whackier, the better... as long as it works.

New innovations will be breaking out everywhere, as will stunning medical advances. The Tiger is associated with healing, amongst other striking qualities, so pharmaceutical breakthroughs are likely to continue and accelerate. And since the Tiger prefers new approaches, alternative treatments and therapies will be explored in more detail, and many found to be effective.

The emphasis on mental health and psychology will also expand, encouraged by Water-enhanced communication at ever deeper and more personal levels.

Water into Gold

Anything and everything to do with water will be worth considering as far as investments go. From deep-sea diving, marine reserves and re-growing endangered coral, to fish farms, cruises and tidal energy – if it's associated with water, good luck will follow. Fancy starting a surf school, miles inland or running swimming lessons for babies? Go for it in 2022.

Huge fortunes will be made, but others lost. Tiger years are financial roller-coasters, and no one can say who will win and who will lose. Yet, the impetus is always onwards and upwards despite a few casualties along the way. So, if you're brave – ride the Tiger!

No Hiding Place

Thieves, conmen, lying politicians, and grasping corporations are likely to be exposed and made to pay in 2022. The Tiger stands for justice and fairness – the kind of fairness that's not necessarily connected to the letter of the law. Wealthy wrong-doers may try to escape retribution by wriggling out of the rules, but it won't work this year. Some surprising names could be hitting the headlines and shamed. Some will even end up in jail. On the other hand, people who've been cheated, ignored, and walked over in the past could suddenly find the tables turned dramatically in their favour. That's justice, Tiger-style.

As the Tiger is also the guardian of children, children's rights will be coming to the fore this year. Expect more fuss about internet exploitation of the young, as well as education and children's mental health issues. Also, youthful voices being raised (particularly around climate change), young opinions taken more seriously, and young talent surging into the spotlight on screen and in the music business.

Dust off those Suitcases

If 2021 was the year of the staycation, 2022 is the year we spread our wings again. The Ox of 2021 was no traveller, but the Tiger is a totally different beast. Tiger years encourage travel and exploration, so 2022 is likely to welcome a big upsurge in foreign holidays. After two consecutive years of confinement at home, it'll seem like half the world is on the move. Businesses connected to tourism are likely to boom, with eco-trips particularly popular, and since this is a Water year, cruises and holidays involving water sports will be bouncing back.

Combining adventure with charity fundraising will also reach new heights, so be prepared for frequent appeals to sponsor family, friends, and work colleagues on their latest challenges for good causes.

Respect the Water Element

Above all, never forget, in all the excitement, that 2022 is also a powerful Water year. Water is going to make itself felt in the next 12 months. At home, watch out for temperamental plumbing, burst pipes, and washing machine mishaps. On a global scale, we could see unusual floods, excessive rainfall, and tsunamis where we least expect them. Just as in 1962, the drive to communicate, accentuated in Water years, could become too intense and lead to disasters around international travel and difficulties in tourist hotspots.

Water is also connected to the emotions, so leaders around the world could suddenly become prone to over-reacting to provocations, real or imagined, or generally behaving in an illogical, over-the-top manner. Let's hope that just as in 1962, they come to their senses and calm down before the situation gets out of hand.

The Tiger Takes the Stage

So, this is likely to be the shape of 2022. Chances are, we haven't quite seen the last of Covid-19, but the focus in this Water year could move unexpectedly from the lungs to the kidneys. The good news is that the Tiger is associated with healing, so new treatments and methods of finally keeping the outbreak under control are likely to manifest.

The Tiger is here to help us all put the pandemic behind us, to move forward and get on with the exciting job of creating a brave new world.

How the Years Got their Names

According to Chinese folklore, there are many explanations as to why the calendar is divided up the way it is. Perhaps the most popular is the story about the supreme Jade Emperor who lives in heaven. He decided to name each year in honour of a different animal and decreed that a race would be run to decide which animals would be chosen, and the order in which they would appear.

Twelve animals arrived to take part. Actually, in one legend there were 13, and included the cat, at the time a great friend of the rat. But the cat was a sleepy creature and asked the rat to wake him in time for the race and in the excitement (or was it by design?) the rat forgot and dashed off leaving the cat fast asleep. The cat missed the race and missed out on getting a year dedicated to his name. Which is why cats have hated rats ever since.

Anyway, as they approached the finish line, the 12 competitors found a wide river blocking their route. The powerful Ox, a strong swimmer, plunged straight in, but the tiny Rat begged to be carried across on his back. Kindly Ox agreed, but when they reached the opposite bank, the wily Rat scampered down Ox's body, jumped off his head and shot across the finish line in first place. Which is why the Rat is the first animal of the Chinese zodiac, followed by the Ox.

The muscular Tiger, weighed down by his magnificent coat, arrived in third place, followed by the non-swimming Rabbit who'd found some rocks downstream and hopped neatly from one to another to reach dry land.

The Emperor was surprised to see the Dragon with his great wings, fly in, in fifth place, instead of the expected first. The Dragon explained that while high up in the sky he saw a village in flames and the people running out of their houses in great distress, so he'd made a detour and employed his rain-making skills (Chinese Dragons can create water as well as fire) to put out the blaze before returning to the race.

In sixth place came the Snake. Clever as the Rat, the Snake had wrapped himself around one of the Horse's hooves and hung on while the Horse swam the river. When the Horse climbed ashore, the Snake slithered off, so startling the Horse that it reared up in alarm, allowing the Snake to slide over the finish line ahead of him.

The Goat, Monkey, and Rooster arrived next at the river. They spotted some driftwood and rope washed up on the shore, so Monkey deftly lashed them together to make a raft and the three of them hopped aboard and floated across. The Goat jumped off first, swiftly followed by Monkey and Rooster. They found they'd beaten the Dog which was unexpected as the Dog was a good swimmer.

It turned out the Dog so enjoyed the water, he'd hung around playing in the shallows emerging only in time to come eleventh. Last of all came the Pig, not the best of swimmers, and further slowed by his decision to pause for a good meal before exerting himself in the current.

And so the wheel of the zodiac was set forevermore, with the Year of the Rat beginning the cycle, followed by the Ox, Tiger, Rabbit, Dragon, Snake, Horse, Goat, Monkey, Rooster, Dog and Pig.

How to Succeed in 2022

So, since 2022 is the Year of the Tiger, how will you fare? Does the Tiger present your astrological animal with opportunities or challenges? As the fable about how the years got their names shows, every one of the astrological animals is resourceful in its own special way. Faced with the daunting prospect of crossing the river, each successfully made it to the other side, even the creatures that could barely swim.

So, whether your year animal gets on easily with the Black Water Tiger, or whether they have to work at their relationship, you can make 2022 a wonderful year to remember.

Chinese Astrology has been likened to a weather forecast. Once you know whether you'll need your umbrella or your suntan lotion, you can step out with confidence and enjoy the trip.

Find Your Chinese Astrology Sign

To find your Chinese sign just look up your birth year in the table below.

Important note: if you were born in January or February, check the dates of the New Year very carefully. The Chinese New Year follows the lunar calendar and the beginning and end dates are not fixed, but vary each year. If you were born before mid-February, your animal sign might actually be the sign of the previous year. For example, 1980 was the year of the Monkey but the Chinese New Year began on February 16 so a person born in January or early February 1980 would belong to the year before – the year of the Goat.

And there's More to it Than That...

In case you're saying to yourself, but surely, how can every person born in the same 365 days have the same personality(?) – you're quite right. The birth year is only the beginning.

Your birth year reflects the way others see you and your basic characteristics, but your month and time of birth are also ruled by the celestial animals – probably different animals from the one that dominates your birth year. The personalities of these other animals modify and add talents to those you acquired with your birth year creature.

The 1920s

5 February 1924 – 24 January 1925 | RAT

25 January 1925 – 12 February 1926 | OX

13 February 1926 – 1 February 1927 | TIGER

2 February 1927 – 22 January 1928 | RABBIT

23 January 1928 – 9 February 1929 | DRAGON

10 February 1929 – 29 January 1930 | SNAKE

The 1930s

30 January 1930 – 16 February 1931 | HORSE

17 February 1931 – 5 February 1932 | GOAT

6 February 1932 – 25 January 1933 | MONKEY

26 January 1933 – 13 February 1934 | ROOSTER

14 February 1934 – 3 February 1935 | DOG

4 February 1935 – 23 January 1936 | PIG

24 January 1936 – 10 February 1937 | RAT

11 February 1937 – 30 January 1938 | OX

31 January 1938 – 18 February 1939 | TIGER

19 February 1939 – 7 February 1940 | RABBIT

The 1940s

8 February 1940 – 26 January 1941 | DRAGON

27 January 1941 – 14 February 1942 | SNAKE

15 February 1942 – 4 February 1943 | HORSE

5 February 1943 – 24 January 1944 | GOAT

25 January 1944 – 12 February 1945 | MONKEY

13 February 1945 – 1 February 1946 | ROOSTER

2 February 1946 – 21 January 1947 | DOG

22 January 1947 – 9 February 1948 | PIG

10 February 1948 – 28 January 1949 | RAT

29 January 1949 – 16 February 1950 | OX

The 1950s

17 February 1950 – 5 February 1951 | TIGER

6 February 1951 – 26 January 1952 | RABBIT

27 January 1952 – 13 February 1953 | DRAGON

14 February 1953 – 2 February 1954 | SNAKE

3 February 1954 – 23 January 1955 | HORSE

24 January 1955 – 11 February 1956 | GOAT

12 February 1956 – 30 January 1957 | MONKEY

31 January 1957 – 17 February 1958 | ROOSTER

18 February 1958 – 7 February 1959 | DOG

8 February 1959 – 27 January 1960 | PIG

The 1960s

28 January 1960 – 14 February 1961 | RAT

15 February 1961 – 4 February 1962 | OX

5 February 1962 – 24 January 1963 | TIGER

25 January 1963 – 12 February 1964 | RABBIT

13 February 1964 – 1 February 1965 | DRAGON

2 February 1965 – 20 January 1966 | SNAKE

21 January 1966 – 8 February 1967 | HORSE

9 February 1967 – 29 January 1968 | GOAT

30 January 1968 – 16 February 1969 | MONKEY

17 February 1969 – 5 February 1970 | ROOSTER

The 1970s

6 February 1970 – 26 January 1971 | DOG

27 January 1971 – 14 February 1972 | PIG

15 February 1972 – 2 February 1973 | RAT

3 February 1973 – 22 January 1974 | OX

23 January 1974 – 10 February 1975 | TIGER

11 February 1975 – 30 January 1976 | RABBIT

31 January 1976 – 17 February 1977 | DRAGON

18 February 1977 – 6 February 1978 | SNAKE

7 February 1978 – 27 January 1979 | HORSE

28 January 1979 – 15 February 1980 | GOAT

The 1980s

16 February 1980 – 4 February 1981 | MONKEY

5 February 1981 – 24 January 1982 | ROOSTER

25 January 1982 – 12 February 1983 | DOG

13 February 1983 – 1 February 1984 | PIG

2 February 1984 – 19 February 1985 | RAT

20 February 1985 – 8 February 1986 | OX

9 February 1986 – 28 January 1987 | TIGER

29 January 1987 – 16 February 1988 | RABBIT

17 February 1988 – 5 February 1989 | DRAGON

6 February 1989 – 26 January 1990 | SNAKE

The 1990s

27 January 1990 – 14 February 1991 | HORSE

15 February 1991 – 3 February 1992 | GOAT

4 February 1992 – 22 January 1993 | MONKEY

23 January 1993 – 9 February 1994 | ROOSTER

10 February 1994 – 30 January 1995 | DOG

31 January 1995 – 18 February 1996 | PIG

19 February 1996 – 7 February 1997 | RAT

8 February 1997 – 27 January 1998 | OX

28 January 1998 – 5 February 1999 | TIGER

6 February 1999 – 4 February 2000 | RABBIT

The 2000s

5 February 2000 – 23 January 2001 | DRAGON

24 January 2001 – 11 February 2002 | SNAKE

12 February 2002 – 31 January 2003 | HORSE

1 February 2003 – 21 January 2004 | GOAT

22 January 2004 – 8 February 2005 | MONKEY

9 February 2005 – 28 January 2006 | ROOSTER

29 January 2006 – 17 February 2007 | DOG

18 February 2007 – 6 February 2008 | PIG

7 February 2008 – 25 January 2009 | RAT

26 January 2009 – 13 February 2010 | OX

The 2010s

14 February 2010 – 2 February 2011 | TIGER

3 February 2011 – 22 January 2012 | RABBIT

23 January 2012 – 9 February 2013 | DRAGON

10 February 2013 – 30 January 2014 | SNAKE

31 January 2014 – 18 February 2015 | HORSE

19 February 2015 – 7 February 2016 | GOAT

8 February 2016 – 27 January 2017 | MONKEY

28 January 2017 – 15 February 2018 | ROOSTER

16 February 2018 – 4 February 2019 | DOG

5 February 2019 – 24 January 2020 | PIG

The 2020s

25 January 2020 – 11 February 2021 | RAT

12 February 2021 – 31 January 2022 | OX

1 February 2022 – 21 January 2023 | TIGER

22 January 2023 – 9 February 2024 | RABBIT

10 February 2024 – 28 January 2025 | DRAGON

29 January 2025 – 16 February 2026 | SNAKE

17 February 2026 – 5 February 2027 | HORSE

6 February 2027 – 25 January 2028 | GOAT

26 January 2028 – 12 February 2029 | MONKEY

13 February 2029 – 2 February 2030 | ROOSTER

CHAPTER 2: THE TIGER

Tiger Years

13 February 1926 – 1 February 1927

31 January 1938 – 18 February 1939

17 February 1950 – 5 February 1951

5 February 1962 – 24 January 1963

23 January 1974 – 10 February 1975

9 February 1986 – 28 January 1987

28 January 1998 – 5 February 1999

14 February 2010 – 2 February 2011

1 February 2022 – 21 January 2023

Natural Element: Wood

Will 2022 be a Golden Year for the Tiger?

Tiger, Tiger, burning bright… Remember that poem? Well, whether you do or do not, that's you this year, Tiger. Your sign always was the King of the beasts, but now you're King of the year as well. In 2022, you're set to be a blazing star. You're in charge, and your philosophy – your values – will set the tone for the next 12 months. The world will be seeing things the way you do in 2022, Tiger, which makes a very exciting change.

You've become so used to your thinking being out of step with everyone else's that it will probably take some getting used to find them agreeing with you all of a sudden. Try not to look so surprised!

There's a huge amount you can achieve this year, Tiger, yet probably one of the first things you'll want to do is dash off on a foreign trip.

Your sign loves to travel, and the restrictions of the past two years have been difficult to bear. Well, in 2022, that's all going to change, and many a Tiger will find themselves living out of a suitcase for weeks on end and loving every minute. You're set to discover new places you've never explored before, possibly never even knew existed, as well as making a welcome return to some old favourites. In fact, you could become so enamoured of one particular haunt that you decide to move there permanently.

Every area of your life is about to expand in a pleasing way. A scheme you started in the last couple of years that couldn't seem to get off the ground is about to sprout wings and zoom. New jobs beckon, and there's a strong possibility you'll be involved in some charitable, environmental, or even medical project.

This could well begin as a hobby or interesting sideline, but the way things are going, it may rapidly overtake your usual job and end up as a whole new career. Quite a few Tigers will be launching into completely different fields in 2022, some of them almost by accident. Yet, once started, there will be no looking back.

Part of all this delightful action is down to the fact that it's your year, Tiger, but there's more to it even than that. In Chinese astrology, Tigers are believed to belong to the Wood element – the symbol of all growing plant life from the humblest blade of grass to the mightiest forest tree. And the one thing Wood needs to flourish and expand is Water. Since 2022 is a Water year, it will be especially beneficial to all Wood creatures. Tigers can expect to enjoy a lot of outside assistance this year and – at times – it will seem as if you have a magic touch.

Yet, despite all the good news, there are bound to be some moments that are not so perfect. According to the Chinese, being ruler of the year does not mean you can rely on wall to wall good fortune. Being in charge brings responsibilities. The boss is expected to deal with difficult situations, difficult people, and at times make unpopular decisions. As well as praise, bosses can attract criticism, back-biting, and resentment. So you need to be prepared, Tiger. It's tough at the top, as they say, but you can cope.

A good place to start would be with the people around you at work. Even though you may be moving on this year, building a strong network will repay the time and effort tenfold. Quite often, this is an area that impatient Tigers neglect because they're so busy concentrating on the important stuff; they haven't got time for trivial chit-chat.

This year the 'trivial stuff' could turn out to be the most important of all in ways you couldn't foresee; so think twice before you dismiss anything. Typical Tigers are not principally motivated by money. You're so magnificent as you are, Tiger, that you have no need for status symbols. Yet, obviously, you wouldn't say 'no' to some extra cash.

The good news is that finances shouldn't be a problem in 2022 – or at least in the sense of money flowing in. The beneficial Water element has a happy knack of washing cash in your direction and of causing your existing income to grow. Look out for pay rises, gifts, and even wins.

Chances are you'll spend the money on even more far-flung trips; but, while you're abroad, a property may catch your eye that proves irresistible. It could prove perfectly possible to uproot Tiger Towers and move them overseas, while still keeping your career ticking over online. Exciting times, Tiger!

What it Means to Be a Tiger

It's a wonderful thing to be a Tiger. Who could not be impressed with the great cat's magnificent striped coat, lithe yet powerful body, and arrogant, swaggering stride? We're all in awe of the Tiger – as well as being pretty scared, too.

In China, the sign is regarded as fortunate and noble. Fortunate because – let's face it – the Tiger owns the jungle and patrols his territory with savage grace; noble because it's believed the Tiger only kills when it's hungry or threatened. (Which may or may not be strictly true.)

Yet, the zodiac Tiger is also a contrary creature. You never know quite where you are with the typical Tiger. With a coat that's neither black nor orange – neither light nor dark – Tigers have two sides to their characters and can switch moods in an instant.

What's more, that striped pelt provides such perfect camouflage in the jungle; Tiger can melt into the shadows and become completely invisible, only to reappear without warning when least expected, to devastating effect.

Other signs instinctively know never to underestimate the Tiger.

Perhaps unsurprisingly, people born under this sign tend to attract good luck. They throw themselves into risky situations and escape unscathed, where others would come badly unstuck.

Tigers are fearless and restless. They like to be on the move and get bored easily. Wonderfully good-looking, Tigers tend to shine in company, and enjoy being surrounded by admirers, as they usually are. While perfectly happy in their own company and not craving attention, Tigers are confident and unfazed by a crowd. They take it as quite natural that other signs seek them out and want to hear their opinions.

The Tiger has a magnetic personality and can be highly entertaining, but they're also surprisingly moody – laughing and joking one minute, then flying into a rage over almost nothing the next. Despite this, the Tiger is very idealistic. Tiger can see what's wrong with the world and wants to put it right. What's more, courageous Tiger is quite prepared to get out there and put the necessary changes into action.

This is the sign of the daring revolutionary. The trouble is, Tigers can become so accustomed to getting away with audacious acts, they forget that – deep down – they're big cats and cats are said to have only nine lives. Push their luck too far, and sooner or later, Tiger can find it runs out.

Sporty and athletic, Tigers love to travel; when they're young, the typical Tiger is likely to want to be off to see the world. Even older Tigers insist on regular holidays and would happily take a sabbatical or 'adult gap year' if possible. Luxury travel or budget breaks, they don't really care as long as they're going somewhere different. They don't even mind going on their own if necessary, as they're independent and self-assured; they are confident they'll find an interesting companion from time to time, along the way, if they need one.

Far too individual to be slaves to fashion, Tigers of both sexes still manage to look stylish and original in a pared-down, sleek sort of way. They can't be bothered with fiddly, fussy details, and they don't need to be because their natural features attract attention effortlessly. Similarly, the Tiger's home is attractive and unusual: full of intriguing objects and trophies that Tiger has collected during their adventures.

At work, if they manage to avoid quarrelling with the boss and walking out – a strong possibility as Tigers hate to be told what to do – Tigers tend to rise to the top of whatever field they happen to be in. But contradictory to the end, the Tiger is just as likely to reach the peak of their profession and then resign to try something new. In business, the Tiger can be creative, innovative, and utterly ruthless to competitors.

Best Jobs for Tiger in 2022

Charity Boss

Environmentalist

Medical Researcher

Scientist

Documentary Maker

Naturalist

Perfect Partners

Cupid's arrow can strike anywhere at any time, of course, but once the novelty of new romance wears off, some relationships are easier to maintain than others. Here's a guide to the Tiger's compatibility with other signs.

Tiger with Tiger

The attraction between these two beautiful people is powerful. They understand each other so well, it's almost like looking in a mirror. They both like to walk on the wild side and will enjoy some exciting adventures together, but their moody interludes could lead to fierce quarrels. This match could be compulsive but stormy.

Tiger with Rabbit

Surprisingly, the Rabbit is not intimidated by Tiger's dangerous aura, and this attitude immediately appeals to Tiger who enjoys a challenge. Rabbit's calm presence and clever way with words keeps Tiger interested, while Rabbit finds Tiger's adventurous tales entertaining. With care, these two could get on well together for years.

Tiger with Dragon

The two biggest personalities in the zodiac would seem bound to clash. After all, these larger than life characters share so many similarities there's a danger they'd compete. Yet a relationship between the Tiger and Dragon often works very well. They understand each other's impulsive natures, but they're also different enough to supply the support the other needs. They'd make a formidable power couple.

Tiger with Snake

Not the best of romances. These two are so fundamentally different that any initial attraction is unlikely to last. Snake likes to bask and conserve energy while Tiger wants to leap right in and race about. Tiger takes in the big picture in a glance and is off to the next challenge while Snake likes to pause, delve beneath the surface, and consider. It wouldn't take long before these two annoy each other.

Tiger with Horse

This athletic pair get on pretty well. They both like physical pursuits, testing their strength out of doors or just enjoying the feel of the wind in their hair and the ground under their feet. True, Horse may not quite understand Tiger's plans for world domination, but it doesn't really matter. Horse is happy to be loyal to such a charismatic partner. As they're both moody, there could be rows, but making up is exciting.

Tiger with Goat

Tiger and Goat don't have a lot in common. While their aims and temperaments are quite different, they are both sociable creatures, and Goat wouldn't mind Tiger attracting all the attention when they're out together. Tiger, in return, would appreciate Goat's lack of jealousy and generosity of spirit. Yet, long-term, they're likely to drift apart as they follow their different interests.

Tiger with Monkey

Tiger can't help being intrigued by sparkling Monkey and Monkey is flattered by such interest. Who wouldn't enjoy being admired by such a fabulous creature? But irrepressible Monkey just can't help teasing and being teased is not a sensation Tiger is familiar with, nor appreciates. Unless the attraction is very strong, these two will wind each other up until they can bear it no longer and part.

Tiger with Rooster

The only feathered creature in the zodiac, the opulence and novelty of Rooster's appearance will draw Tiger like a magnet. What's more, deep down they are both quite serious-minded types so, on one level, they'll have much to share. Yet, despite this, they're not really on the same wavelength, and misunderstandings will keep recurring. Could be hard work.

Tiger with Dog

While not exactly opposites, these two are different enough to intrigue each other yet similar enough in basic outlook to get on well. Both Tiger and Dog are idealistic and uninterested in material gain yet where Dog can be nervous, Tiger's bold; and where Tiger attracts controversy, Dog will be loyal. This partnership could be lasting and valuable.

Tiger with Pig

Carefree Pig will love to bask in Tiger's impressive aura, while Tiger will feel good about protecting this charming but unworldly creature. They enjoy each other's company and Tiger, so focused on lofty matters will find Pig's compulsive shopping too trivial to worry about. This couple could do well together as long as Pig's fondness for cosy nights in doesn't make Tiger feel trapped.

Tiger with Rat

Sleek and clever Rat can easily attract Tiger's attention because the intelligent Tiger loves witty conversation. Yet these two are not natural partners. Tiger's not interested in Rat's latest bargain and has no wish to talk about it while Rat doesn't share Tiger's passion for changing the world. Still, if they can agree to step back and not get in each other's way, they could reach a good understanding.

Tiger with Ox

Not an easy match. Ox and Tiger could be on different planets. Fiery Tiger doesn't frighten Ox, and Tiger may admire Ox's strong, good looks and sincere nature, but they both need different things from life. Tiger wants to dash about creating big changes, while Ox reckons you get more done by buckling down where you happen to be and attending to the details. Clashes could abound.

Tiger Love 2022 Style

Chances are, you're already accustomed to being the star of the show, Tiger. After all, Tigers combine natural good looks, feline grace, and a magnetic air of confidence that attracts attention wherever they go. To be honest, you probably take it for granted and don't even realise other signs don't share your amazing luck.

Well, this year, you can strut about like a rock idol. Even though you don't get a special uniform when you're King or Queen of the year, the other signs sense your authority, and are drawn to you like never before.

At work, in the pub, on the train... wherever you happen to be, romantic encounters could present themselves. Naturally, you will make the most of the fun, providing you have time.

Tigers tend to put saving the world before nurturing their love life. Yet this year, Tiger, you could meet a fellow traveller who shares your interests and before you know it, you've decided to pool your resources and everything else as well.

Though you hate to be tied down, this match will feel more like spreading your wings together, which is as near perfection as any Tiger could wish for.

Attached Tigers will have to work harder than usual to pay attention to their partners, unless of course those partners are remarkably understanding or already devoted to the same causes. Some Tiger partners are busy doing their own thing, of course, and remain perfectly happy to snuggle up with their big cat on an almost part-time basis. Others, though, would prefer a more conventional arrangement. Clever Tigers who value the relationship will make an extra effort to include their loved one in their adventures this year.

Secrets of Success in 2022

Right, well, the world's your oyster this year, Tiger. Almost everything you touch will turn out well, or at least get off to a strong start. People will tend to say 'yes' to you in 2022. In some cases, this will be so surprising you'll think you've misheard. You've become so used to your brainwaves being dismissed as impractical, too expensive, or just not suitable right now, that you expect to be turned down when you try to make changes.

Bearing this in mind, maybe you should be slightly more cautious about voicing some of your more revolutionary ideas. If they're accepted, as they may well be, you'll be the one required to pick up the pieces in a later year if it all goes horribly wrong under the next zodiac sign.

Ask yourself, too, if you really, truly want that fabulous job you're about to apply for. Tigers crave excitement and tend to leap from project to project, role to role, partly for the sheer challenge of doing something different. Normal restrictions in other years tend to prevent you from taking on too much, Tiger, but the brakes are off in 2022. Chances are you'll be given any job you want, so be quite sure you'll actually enjoy doing the tasks involved, or you'll end up letting people down.

Finally, don't get too carried away with your spending just because a lot of cash is coming your way. You'll need some next year, too! And, above all, don't let your success go to your head. Proud Tigers can end up appearing arrogant. Not a good look if you hope to have some friends in 2023!

The Tiger Year at a Glance

January – Ox fatigue is setting in, and you're probably bored, Tiger. Yet you can sense the change in the air. Excitement is growing.

February – Wow! You're on top of the world all of a sudden. Nothing much has changed, yet you can feel everything's changing.

March – You're branching out in every direction. Job offers, travel plans, people to meet, places to go…

April – An authority figure at work irritates, yet suddenly you see a way to bypass them and come out on top.

May – A promising romance turns sour as your new partner expects more of you than you're happy to give. Probably not a keeper Tiger.

June – A major project is coming to fruition. You put everything else on hold and dive in.

July – Travel for work or pleasure is on the cards, which is just the way you like it. Start packing.

August – Everyone seems to be on holiday right now, just when you're gearing up for action. Still, if they're not around, you can do things your way.

September – A dazzling newcomer catches your eye. The two of you get on brilliantly. Sparks are flying.

October – You're flavour of the month at work. Promotion, a pay rise, or both are on offer.

November – An extravagant person holds you up. They don't seem to understand the need for budgeting. Extreme patience is required.

December – Traditional Christmas? Not necessarily Tiger. Festivities on the beach beckon this year.

Lucky colours for 2022: Black, Silver, Turquoise

Lucky numbers for 2022: 4, 8

CHAPTER 3: THE RABBIT

Rabbit Years

2 February 1927 – 22 January 1928

19 February 1939 – 7 February 1940

6 February 1951 – 26 January 1952

25 January 1963 – 12 February 1964

11 February 1975 – 30 January 1976

29 January 1987 – 16 February 1988

6 February 1999 – 4 February 2000

3 February 2011 – 22 January 2012

22 January 2023 – 9 February 2024

Natural Element: Wood

Will 2022 be a Golden Year for the Rabbit?

Time to shape up, Rabbit. 2022 will be a fantastic year for you, but you've got to get yourself out of your burrow and into the action. The whole world has been in turmoil for these last two years of the Rat and then the Ox, and many Rabbits have sensibly kept their heads down, paws over their ears, and carried on one cautious step at a time.

Now, though, everything's changed, and that includes the Rabbit's prospects. Tiger years are sometimes a little daunting for Rabbits. Not because Rabbit and Tiger don't get on – strangely enough, they're quite good friends. It's just that Tiger energy is so strong; it can all get a bit overwhelming for the sensitive bunny. Everything can seem too fast, too loud, too much.

Yet, of all the Tiger years, 2022 is probably the best for the Rabbit since it's a Black Tiger Year ruled by the Water element. Black Tiger is a Tiger with the rough edges smoothed off and softened; a far easier beast for Rabbit to handle.

Not only is the Black Tiger more sympathetic to the Rabbit's point of view, but the Water element of the year is also especially beneficial. This is because – like the Tiger – the Rabbit is believed to belong to the Wood family of creatures. Wood in Chinese astrology doesn't just represent logs and timber furniture, it's a symbol of all green plants and epitomises the powerful impulses of growth and expansion.

Since the Tiger and the Rabbit both belong to the Wood family, they have a surprising amount in common, but they also require Water to reach their full potential.

The Water element of 2022 will help the Rabbit fortunes to grow and career prospects to blossom. Projects that had come almost to a standstill during the Ox year will suddenly sprout new shoots and leap back into life.

If you're typical of your sign, you didn't do badly last year, Rabbit, but there was something about the energy that made you a bit on edge. You're not the kind to take big risks at the best of times, but during the reign of the Ox you felt obliged to be extra cautious. That's probably because the element of the year was Metal which is viewed as unfriendly by Rabbits, suggestive as it is of sharp implements and scary cutting blades. Best keep well out of the way of that lot!

The conditions couldn't be more different in 2022. With Water pushing you on, you can afford to try out new ideas, experiment with business ventures, or make career moves that are normally beyond your comfort zone. The only aspect that could give you sleepless nights is the speed and force of any changes in which you might dip a tentative toe.

The Water element unleashed by the Tiger is more like the kind of towering wave adored by surfers than a gentle ripple across a sunlit pond. Whatever you start could suddenly sweep you up and carry you away much faster than you ever imagined.

Yet, this isn't necessarily a bad thing. It's just that it's nerve-wracking for the typical Rabbit temperament.

If you can overcome your doubts, Rabbit, it looks as if you could be given charge of a very special project in 2022. In fact, if it goes well, you could find yourself on the path to fame and fortune.

Perhaps this is something you began last year, or maybe it's a new venture, but whatever it turns out to be, seize the opportunity and run with it. It will lead you somewhere very interesting indeed.

With all this excitement surrounding your career, you'll need to counterbalance the thrills with some calm time at home. If anything, home and family are going to be even more important to you in 2022. It looks like a family wedding could take you all by surprise, and a new baby will delight everyone. Keep an eye on older relatives, too. The Tiger is reckoned to be a sign that improves health, but with all the Water sloshing about, emotions could be running high – particularly among more vulnerable members of the family. You may be called upon to help and to use your excellent communication skills to explain things.

Some sort of big family holiday is very likely, too, possibly associated with that wedding, and if you can manage to make it in a watery setting or on board a ship, it will be especially lucky.

So get out there, Rabbit, and make 2022 count!

What it Means to Be a Rabbit

We all love Rabbits, don't we? After the possibly dull Ox, and terrifying Tiger, the soft and pretty Rabbit seems like a welcome relief. We can all relate to the Rabbit. Big brown eyes, powder puff-tail, cute little quivering nose, and an endearing way of hopping neatly around – nobody could take offence at the Rabbit.

In fact, nobody could feel threatened by the Rabbit in any way unless they happen to be a carrot, or a salad vegetable.

Yet, in the West, not all zodiac Rabbits are proud of their sign. They believe it suggests vulnerability and lack of drive. In the East, however, the Rabbit is appreciated for some very important qualities.

Like the Rat, Rabbits are brilliant survivors; they thrive and colonise in all manner of difficult terrains; but, unlike the Rat, they manage to do this – mostly – without enraging or disgusting anyone, bar a few irritated farmers.

For all their cuddly looks, these are tough little creatures, frequently under-estimated. It's no accident that in the Chinese calendar, the defenceless, non-swimming Rabbit still manages to cross the river in fourth place, way ahead of stronger, abler creatures with seemingly much more going for them.

People born under this sign are never flashy or loud. Enter a crowded room, and the Rabbit wouldn't be the first person you notice. Yet, after a while, a stylish, immaculately-turned-out character would draw your eye. Classy and understated with perfect hair and graceful gestures – the typical Rabbit. This effortlessly polished aura is a gift. A Rabbit can emerge soaked to the skin from a rainstorm in a muddy field and within minutes appear clean, unruffled, and co-ordinated. Even Rabbits don't know how they do it. They're not even aware they *are* doing it.

Rabbits are refined with cultured tastes. They love beautiful things and art of all kinds, and hate to be surrounded by untidiness and disorder. Harmony is very important to the Rabbit – both visually and emotionally. People born in Rabbit years are sensitive in every way. They hate loud noises, loud voices, heavy traffic, and general ugliness. Quarrels can actually make them ill.

Yet this loathing of discord doesn't mean the Rabbit retires from the world. Rabbits somehow manage to end up near the centre of the action and tend to walk away with what they want, without appearing to have made any visible effort to get it.

Softly-spoken Rabbits are natural diplomats. Discreet and tactful, they can always find the right words, the perfect solutions to keep everybody happy. In fact, their powers of persuasion are so sophisticated that people usually do what Rabbit wants in the belief it's their own idea. This approach is so successful that Rabbit can't understand why other signs resort to argument and challenge, when so much more can be achieved through quiet conversation and compromise.

Rabbits tend to be brilliant strategists. When other egos get too distracted, jockeying for position and trying to be in charge for the task in hand, Rabbit deftly assesses the situation and has a plan worked out before the others have even agreed an agenda. Outwardly modest, Rabbits rarely admit to being ambitious, so they often end up being underestimated. Yet, privately, Rabbits can be single-minded and determined; even ruthless at times. These qualities, combined with their diplomatic skills and calm efficiency, seem to propel them smoothly to the top of whatever profession they've chosen.

Rabbits love their homes, which naturally are as beautiful and harmonious as they are. Home is a sanctuary and Rabbits take a lot of pleasure in choosing just the right pieces and décor to make their special place perfect, but in a comfortable way. Tidiness comes easily to them, and they can bring order to chaos quickly and neatly with the minimum of fuss. They enjoy entertaining – preferably small, informal gatherings of good friends – and they make wonderful hosts. Since they are such agreeable types, they're popular with everyone and a Rabbit's invitation to dinner is accepted with eagerness.

When life is calm and secure, the Rabbit is perfectly happy to stay in one place. These types are not desperate for novelty though they do enjoy a relaxing holiday. Extreme sports are unlikely to appeal, but gentle exercise in beautiful surroundings soothes their nerves, and if they can take in an art gallery or a historic church followed by a delicious meal, they'd be truly contented bunnies.

Best Jobs for Rabbit 2022

Fashion model

Counsellor

Diplomat

Business Consultant

Beauty Therapist

Interior Designer

Estate Agent

Personal Shopper

Perfect Partners

Cupid's arrow can strike anywhere at any time, of course, but once the novelty of new romance wears off, some relationships are easier to maintain than others. Here's a guide to the Rabbit's compatibility with other signs.

Rabbit with Rabbit

These two gorgeous creatures look like they're made for each other. Their relationship will always be calm, peaceful, and unruffled and it goes without saying that their home could grace a glossy magazine. Yet though they never argue, the willingness of both partners to compromise could end up with neither ever quite doing what they want. Ultimately, they may find the spark goes out.

Rabbit with Dragon

Dragon is such a larger than life character Rabbit could feel overwhelmed at times. Also, the Dragon can be rather noisy and over-dramatic which would get on Rabbit's nerves. Yet they each admire the other's good points. If they could live next door to each other instead of under the same roof, a long-term relationship might work.

Rabbit with Snake

This subtle pair could make a good combination. They both understand the value of working behind the scenes and neither has any desire to wear themselves out on endless adventures. They share a love of art, fine things, and quiet pleasures, and they both enjoy an orderly home. These two could settle down very happily together.

Rabbit with Horse

This could be tricky. It's fairly unlikely that Horse and Rabbit would ever end up on a date but if they did, and there was a strong attraction, it could lead to a love/hate relationship. Rabbit's neat and tidy ways would enrage Horse and Horse's unpredictable moods and over-the-top reactions would annoy Rabbit. Soon, Horse is likely to bolt for the hills or Rabbit retreat to its burrow.

Rabbit with Goat

Happy-go-lucky Goat is very appealing to Rabbit, particularly as deep down Rabbit is a bit of a worrier. They're both sociable without needing to be the centre of attention and would be happy to people-watch for hours and then cheerfully compare notes afterwards. Goat is tolerant of Rabbit's need for some regular alone time to recharge too, so this couple could be a successful match.

Rabbit with Monkey

Mercurial Monkey doesn't really 'get' Rabbit. The Monkey can appreciate how well Rabbit operates and sees this approach gets good results, but it's all too picky and slow for Monkey. Rabbit, on the other hand, is amused by Monkey's quick wit and clever ways but deplores Monkey's slapdash, sometimes devious tactics. Very unlikely to work out.

Rabbit with Rooster

Another difficult match. However unfair it seems, Rooster comes over as loud, boastful, and uncouth to Rabbit while Rabbit appears dull, staid, and insufficiently admiring of Rooster's fine feathers to appeal to Rooster. These two just can't see below the surface of the other, and it would be surprising if they ended up together. Only to be considered by the very determined.

Rabbit with Dog

Despite the fact that in the outside world Rabbit could easily end up as Dog's dinner, the astrological pair get on surprisingly well. Dog appreciates Rabbit's careful, efficient ways and soft voice, while Rabbit admires Dog's energy and good intentions. Dog's lack of interest in the finer points of interior design might try Rabbit's patience, but with a little work these two could reach an understanding.

Rabbit with Pig

Pig is not quite as interested in fine dining as Rabbit being as happy to scoff a burger as a Cordon Bleu creation, but their shared love of the good things in life makes these two happy companions. Once again, Pig's spending habits might irritate Rabbit, but not too much as Rabbit is quite willing to splurge on lovely things for the home. A relationship would work well.

Rabbit with Rat

Rat finds Rabbit intriguing. Here is an attractive, stylish creature that doesn't feel the need to be pushy or take centre stage yet somehow manages to be at the heart of things, while Rabbit is flattered and entertained by witty Rat's attention. These two respect each other but long-term, Rat could be too overpowering unless they both agree to give each other space.

Rabbit with Ox

Ox finds Rabbit rather cute and appealing. Whether male or female there's something about Rabbit's inner fluffiness that brings out Ox's highly-developed protective instincts. Rabbit meanwhile loves the Ox's reassuring presence, and the sense of security Ox provides. These two could get on very well together as long as refined Rabbit can overlook Ox's occasional down-to-earth – Rabbit might say 'coarse' – observations.

Rabbit with Tiger

Surprisingly the Rabbit is not intimidated by Tiger's dangerous aura and this attitude immediately appeals to Tiger who enjoys a challenge. Rabbit's calm presence and clever way with words keeps Tiger interested, while Rabbit finds Tiger's adventurous tales entertaining. With care, these two could get on well together for years.

Rabbit Love 2022 Style

As we lurched from lockdown to lockdown last year, naughty single Rabbits didn't get the chance to frolic in their normal, carefree manner. Well, the Tiger's got the answer to that in 2022! The door's been thrown wide open, and you're being encouraged to hop out there and play.

Despite Rabbit's elegant and fastidious appearance, single Rabbits are extremely successful when it comes to romance and beguiling potential partners. The brash, showy signs might attract a lot of attention but – at the end of the evening – it's often quiet Rabbit that leaves with the partner of their choice.

Well, get back to the party, and keep on doing what you used to do, Rabbit! You're going to be more popular than ever. Single Rabbits are destined to be lucky in love this year, but despite that, may not be ready to make lasting commitments in 2022. After being restrained for so long, you'll probably want to enjoy a few months of exhilarating freedom and frivolity.

Attached Rabbits, on the other hand, may feel even more inspired than usual to expand, expand, expand. That impulse could take the form of more baby bobtails in the household, extensions to the home, buying up more land, or even investing in a second property. As long as your partner agrees with these schemes, the two of you will enjoy blissful evenings designing your brand new future.

Secrets of Success in 2022

Tiger years are all about growth and prosperity, Rabbit, and there's absolutely no reason why you shouldn't enjoy your fair share. You've got a lot going for you in 2022, including (as mentioned earlier) a project that could lead to fame and fortune.

Yet, to capitalise on your amazing prospects, you need to be disciplined. Remember *at all times* the nature of the energy this year, and don't allow it to run away with you. The pace is fast – which is not ideal for Rabbit sensitivities. If you're not careful, the stress of meeting unrealistic deadlines or simply attempting to keep up with the others could lead you to rush or skimp your usual painstaking processes. This would be a big mistake.

Grand plans could fall apart when careless errors come to light. There's also a suggestion that – this year – there will be more to certain situations or people in your orbit than meets the eye.

If you try to speed on through, you might fail to notice a problem lurking just beneath the surface.

What's more, all this dash and pressure is quite unnecessary. So keep calm, Rabbit. Refuse to be hurried. Keep on doing what you know should be done, examine the small print, and you can celebrate a wonderfully successful year.

The Rabbit Year at a Glance

January – Things are calming down in the Rabbit household this month. Take advantage of a quiet time to recharge your batteries.

February – Hopefully, you are now refreshed because the pace is hotting up. An intriguing offer comes your way.

March – You've got a spring in your step and a new love interest on the horizon. Don't forget the day job, though.

April – An authority figure is fizzing with new ideas. Can you cope with rearranging your schedule? Probably wise to try.

May – Things are going well. Your career is flying, and everyone thinks you're wonderful. Try not to smirk.

June – A moody person, either at work or home, is being irritating. No point in arguing. Keep clear or steer around them.

July – You long for the great outdoors. Take a holiday if possible or fix some weekends away.

August – Inspiration strikes. You've got a brilliant idea, and now's the time to share it.

September – Colleagues are sluggish after the holidays. You don't like it, but boss Rabbits might have to chivvy and scold.

October – A cash windfall has your name on it. Time to indulge in a little luxury.

November – Romance is going well. Domestic bliss is appealing. Think cosy dinners by the fire and lots of candles.

December – It might be the festive season, but your career is still firing on all cylinders. If you can, leave the shopping to someone else.

Lucky colours for 2022: Silver, Purple, Yellow

Lucky numbers for 2022: 5, 7

CHAPTER 4: THE DRAGON

Dragon Years

23 January 1928 – 9 February 1929

8 February 1940 – 26 January 1941

27 January 1952 – 13 February 1953

13 February 1964 – 1 February 1965

31 January 1976 – 17 February 1977

17 February 1988 – 5 February 1989

5 February 2000 – 23 January 2001

23 January 2012 – 9 February 2013

10 February 2024 – 28 January 2025

Natural Element: Wood

Will 2022 be a Golden Year for the Dragon?

Congratulations, Dragon, you've made it through 2021's Ox year without (hopefully) incinerating anyone with one puff of your impatient, fiery breath. This is especially impressive because, as the Ox reign drew to a close, the cumulative effect of months and months of inching along like a snail must have driven you to almost pull out your claws in frustration.

So, you'll be thrilled to hear all that's about to change from February 1st, when the Tiger leaps into your life like a jolt of electricity.

By now, you probably don't even care whether the Tiger brings good fortune or bad... as long as there's relief from the tedium. As an action-oriented Dragon, you can bear almost anything except boredom, and at the moment – if you're typical of your sign – you're so BORED!!!

Well, you'll be delighted to hear that 2022 is certainly not going to be boring. What's more, the Tiger is set to bring you a great many goodies. Dragon careers are going to soar to new heights, and cash is likely to be flowing in right behind.

Yet, don't go thinking you can sit back and watch all that good luck pour to you like waves rolling ashore on an incoming tide. There are going to be ups and downs and the odd tricky situation to disentangle.

The reason for this is that you and the Tiger have a feisty relationship. You're both members of the Wood family of zodiac creatures – celestial cousins, as it were – so the Tiger will always support you. Yet you're both regal, dominant types. The Tiger may be the Chinese King of beasts, but the Dragon is the symbol of the Emperor.

The pair of you are bold, brash, fearless leaders, and each thinks they should be in charge. The struggle for supremacy is forever unresolved.

As a result, you get on brilliantly together until you fall out in a spectacular clash. But family's family, and whatever happens, you have each other's backs. So, in a Tiger year, the Dragon will prosper, but Tiger makes you work for it. Challenges will be thrown in your path simply so you can learn from them and grow stronger.

Oddly enough, the typical Dragon doesn't mind this at all. They rather prefer it that way, in fact. Dragon would much rather earn success by clever strategy and sheer talent than by winning the lottery. The one thing no Dragon can resist is a challenge.

In 2022, projects begun the previous year which seemed to be taking forever to make some sort of impression will finally have lift-off. While all Dragon interests, both new and old, will develop and expand.

The Wood energy is all about growth – both upwards and outwards – and Dragon fortunes will do the same right now. The beneficial trend is enhanced this year by the fact the element of 2022 is Water – which is traditionally associated with nourishing and nurturing Wood. That means the Wood family is particularly favoured this year.

Tiger's influence makes this Water-energy particularly strong right now, which can be overwhelming for more delicate signs, but the robust Dragon cheerfully weathers any storm. Dragon finds it exhilarating, in fact.

Basically, the whole tone and pace of 2022 is much more Dragon's style. Buoyed by returning optimism, Dragon's phenomenal energy surges into new ambitions; many a Dragon will start their own business (possibly more than one), move house, change jobs and generally transform their lives in every way they can dream up.

This could be the year, too, when the Dragon is inspired by Tiger's passion for all things green and decides to do something flamboyant for the environment. Whether it's tackling a Marathon – dressed as a dragon, natch – planting an eco-forest, or buying an organic farm, Dragons will be doing their bit for nature as lavishly as they can afford.

And talking of finances, fictional Dragons are renowned for their hoards of treasure. Well, in 2022, most human Dragons will get the chance to increase their hoards quite substantially – probably through a combination of earnings delayed during the year of the Ox plus lucrative new ventures begun now.

Finally, Dragons can look forward to a great deal of travelling in 2022. There's nothing Dragons enjoy more than flying away at regular intervals and, this year, there's nothing to stop you. Yet, the trips are more likely to be work-related than holidays. Still, it matters not to the typical Dragon. They don't much care where they go as long as they go!

What it Means to Be a Dragon

To be honest, Dragon, it's not really fair. Your sign has so many advantages. When you're on good form, your personality is so dazzling the other signs need sunglasses.

The only mythical creature in the celestial cycle, in China the Dragon is associated with the Emperor and revered as a symbol of protection, power, and magnificence. No New Year celebration would be complete without the colourful Dragon, dancing through the streets, twisting and turning, and banishing evil spirits.

The Dragon is regarded as the most fortunate of signs and every couple hopes for a Dragon baby. A child born in a Dragon year is believed to bring good luck to the whole family and, to this day, the birth rate tends to rise about 5% in the Chinese community in Dragon years.

Dragons are usually strong, healthy, and blessed with enormous self-confidence and optimism. Even if they're not conventionally good-looking, they stand out in a crowd. They're charismatic with magnetic personalities, formidable energy, and people look up to them. Dragons are so accustomed to attention, they rarely question why this should be the case. It just seems like the natural way of the world.

These people think BIG. They're visionaries, bubbling with original new ideas, and their enthusiasm is so infectious, their optimism so strong, they easily inspire others. Without even trying, Dragons are born leaders and happily sweep their teams of followers into whatever new venture they've just dreamed up.

The only downside to this is that Dragons are easily bored. Trivial matters – such as details – irritate them, and they're keen to rush on to the next challenge before they've quite finished the first.

With a good second in command, who can attend to the picky minutiae, all could be well. If not, Dragon's schemes can go spectacularly wrong. Yet it hardly seems to matter. The Dragon ascribes to the theory that you have to fail your way to success. Setbacks are quickly forgotten as Dragon launches excitedly into the next adventure and quite often – given the Dragon's good luck – this works.

People born under this sign often receive success and wealth, yet they are not materialistic. They're generous and kind in an absent-minded way, and care far more about having a worthy goal than any rewards it might bring. And it is vital for the Dragon to have a goal. A Dragon without a goal is a sad, dispirited creature – restless and grumpy.

Even if it's not large, the Dragon home gives the impression of space and light. Dragons hate to feel confined in any way. They like to look out the window and see lots of sky and have clear, uncluttered surfaces around them, even if it's difficult for Dragons to keep them that way.

Yet the Dragon home could have a curiously un-lived-in feel. This is because the Dragon regards home as a lair – a comfortable base from which to plan the next project, rather than a place to spend a lot of time.

Dragons love to travel, but they don't really mind where they go as long as it's different and interesting. Yet, despite so much going for them, Dragons often feel misunderstood. Their impatience with trivia extends to the irritating need for tact and diplomacy at times. Dragon doesn't get this. If Dragon has something to say, they say it. Why waste time dressing it up in fancy words they think? But then people get upset, and Dragon is baffled. It's not always easy being a Dragon.

Best Jobs for Dragon

Prime Minister/President

Film Star

Campaigner

Managing Director

Explorer

Editor

Judge

Perfect Partners

Cupid's arrow can strike anywhere at any time, of course, but once the novelty of new romance wears off, some relationships are easier to maintain than others. Here's a guide to the Dragon's compatibility with other signs.

Dragon with Dragon

When Dragon meets Dragon, onlookers tend to take a step back and hold their breath. These two are a combustible mix – they either love each other or loathe each other. They are so alike it could go either way. Both dazzling in their own orbits, they can't fail to notice the other's charms, but since they both need to be centre stage, things could get competitive. With give and take and understanding this match could work well, but it won't be easy.

Dragon with Snake

Surprisingly, this couple gets along beautifully. Snake's elegant appearance and quick but subtle mind intrigues Dragon, while Snake admires Dragon's success and endless energy. Snake has no need to battle for the limelight and is quite happy to sit back and support Dragon's schemes from the comfort of a stylish sofa. Which is all the encouragement Dragon needs.

Dragon with Horse

The athletic Horse is pretty good at keeping up with dashing Dragon. And Dragon appreciates a partner who enjoys getting out and about as much as Dragon does. Yet Horse might grow weary of Dragon's constant new projects and resent having to be involved. Horse likes to go off and do Horsey things at frequent intervals which Dragon tends to view as disloyal. This relationship could get fiery.

Dragon with Goat

Goat tends to baffle the busy Dragon. Dragon can see Goat is the creative type but can't understand why Goat doesn't appear to be working very hard when so much could be achieved. In fact, if they stayed together long enough, Dragon could help Goat make the most of many talents, but it's unlikely either of them can sustain enough interest for this to happen.

Dragon with Monkey

These two are likely to hit it off immediately. Each is attracted to the other's intelligence and lively presence, and Dragon's exuberance doesn't overwhelm hyperactive Monkey. What's more, though they both enjoy being surrounded by a crowd, Monkey only wants to make people laugh while Dragon hopes to inspire them to a cause. There is no conflict, so this couple can help each other to go far.

Dragon with Rooster

A Dragon and Rooster pairing will always attract attention. These two are both gorgeous beings and love to be surrounded by admirers. They will probably enjoy going out together and being seen as a couple, but in the long-term, they may not be able to provide the kind of support each secretly needs.

Entertaining for a while but probably not a lasting relationship.

Dragon with Dog

Not the easiest of combinations. Down-to-earth Dog can't see what all the fuss is about when it comes to Dragons. Unimpressed by glamour and irritated by what seems to Dog the gullibility of Dragon admirers, Dog can't be bothered to find out more. Dragon meanwhile is hurt by Dog's lack of interest. Great determination would be needed to make this work.

Dragon with Pig

While Dragon and Pig might seem to be opposites, the two of them can create a surprisingly contented relationship. Pig is quite happy for Dragon to fly around doing exciting things as long as Pig is not expected to do much more than admire profusely. Dragon appreciates Pig's uncritical support and makes allowances for Pig's lack of stamina. This couple could live in harmony.

Dragon with Rat

This couple is usually regarded as a very good match. They have much in common being action-loving, excitement-seeking personalities who hate to be bored. It takes a lot to dazzle Rat, but the Dragon's glamorous aura proves irresistible, while Dragon loves to be admired, so each enjoys being with the other. There could be the odd power struggle as these two are both strong characters but the magnetism is so intense they usually kiss and make up.

Dragon with Ox

Chalk and cheese though this pair may appear to be, there's a certain fascination between them. Ox may not approve of Dragon's showy manner but recognises Dragon's good intentions, while Dragon admires Ox's strength of character and gift for completing tasks. If each could find a way to tolerate the other's wildly different lifestyles, they might be good for each other but, long-term, Dragon's hectic pace might wear down even the Ox's legendary stamina.

Dragon with Tiger

The two biggest personalities in the zodiac would seem bound to clash. After all, these larger than life characters share so many similarities there's a danger they'd compete. Yet a relationship between the Tiger and Dragon often works well. They understand each other's impulsive natures, but they're also different enough to supply the support the other needs. They'd make a formidable power couple.

Dragon with Rabbit

Dragon is such a larger than life character, Rabbit could feel overwhelmed at times. Also, the Dragon can be rather noisy and over-dramatic, which would get on Rabbit's nerves. Yet they each admire the other's good points. If they could live next door to each other instead of under the same roof, a long-term relationship might work.

Dragon Love 2022 Style

Well, you can't really go wrong this year, Dragon. You're a breathtaking sight at the best of times, and your charisma is legendary, but now – after people have been stuck at home for so long – your appearance back on the party scene is positively dazzling. You only have to enter a room to have admirers flocking.

Some signs might be fazed, but not yours. Dragons adore the attention and find it quite natural. Invitations will be showering all over you this year. You can pick and choose the most fun and hold court in a variety of settings to your heart's content.

The odd thing is, despite being so popular, Dragons don't particularly want to play the field as far as romance is concerned. They're quite happy to entertain the crowd for hours then go home with one quiet and understanding partner at the end of the evening.

This year you'll be spoiled for choice, Dragon. In fact, the trickiest part will be deciding which date to accept.

Attached Dragons have a different challenge to negotiate. Dragon partners will be ready for romance and looking forward to long-postponed candlelit meals *a deux*, while Dragon can't wait to get back on the party circuit. Compromise, think quality-couple-time, and all will be well.

Secrets of Success in 2022

The last thing you probably want to hear, Dragon, after all you've been through, is to restrain yourself. Yet that's your key to success this year. You're destined to do extremely well in 2022. The pressures and restrictions that have been holding you back for so long are melting away and this is your chance, finally, to spread your wings.

Yes, of course you're being encouraged to get out there and seize every opportunity, to be bold and daring and make things happen. Follow your dream, in fact.

All that is true. The trouble is, Dragon, that your enthusiasm takes hold and you go too far at times. Your strength is amazing, and you can achieve a great deal. Yet, in your optimistic way, you tend to overestimate what you can manage.

The danger this year is that you'll say 'yes' to too many projects. You're so excited by all the shiny new things on offer in 2022, you're tempted to accept them all. Chances are, though, you just can't cope with such a workload. If you're not careful, you'll end up ruining the lot and your reputation along with it.

So, if you really want to make the most of your good fortune, count to ten before you take on anything. Examine it carefully and then be selective. Less is more this year, Dragon, or rather, think quality rather than quantity and the future really will be golden.

The Dragon Year at a Glance

January – A corner has been turned. You can feel it. Good times are coming. You can hardly wait.

February – The Tiger year starts with a surprising job opportunity. Consider it carefully.

March – There's a lot of spring cleaning and renovating happening in your orbit. Irritating, but you are happy to be on the move.

April – A project is starting to take off in an exciting way. A rival may appear, but you can see them off.

May – Supporters are out in force, and you're doing well. Cash is increasing. Pay rise or winnings? Either way, don't splurge yet.

June – Travel trips are enticing. Business or pleasure or both combined? You might as well go with the flow and enjoy.

July – Someone in your circle comes over all arty. It may not be your thing, but make them feel good. An event proves surprisingly useful.

August – You're ready to launch a great idea. It's ambitious, but your efforts are appreciated right now. Go for it.

September – A partner, business, or romance is wobbling over a previous promise. Be patient. They'll see sense.

October – An obstructive person is being critical. Recheck your side of things. Do they have a point… or are they just picky?

November – Celebrations all around as your team enjoys success. All down to you, of course, but don't hog the limelight.

December – Christmas is coming, and you're feeling generous. Wait until they see what you've bought them!

Lucky colours for 2022: White, Black, Orange

Lucky numbers for 2022: 1, 5, 2

CHAPTER 5: THE SNAKE

Snake Years

10 February 1929 – 29 January 1930

27 January 1941 – 14 February 1942

14 February 1953 – 2 February 1954

2 February 1965 – 20 January 1966

18 February 1977 – 6 February 1978

6 February 1989 – 26 January 1990

24 January 2001 – 11 February 2002

10 February 2013 – 30 January 2014

29 January 2025 – 16 February 2026

Natural Element: Fire

Will 2022 be a Golden Year for the Snake?

As the new year dawns, Snake, you should be finding yourself surveying a whole new scene. Last year, if you're typical of your sign, you made some major changes, so 2022 will bring you the perfect opportunity to consolidate your gains, enjoy your success, and plan your next clever move.

All around you, other signs will be branching out, attempting to expand and generally breaking new ground. You're more likely to wonder why they're wearing themselves out in such a frantic manner. Few Snakes will be tempted to follow their example. And this year, for you, Snake, your instincts are spot on.

The most significant Snake moves were made in 2021; therefore, it would be unwise to carry on attempting more and more changes while last year's haven't yet had the chance to bed in. That's a recipe for bringing the whole newly-built structure crashing down.

During 2022, wise Snakes will *quietly* build on their successes, gently iron out any glitches, add a little polish here and there, and generally give their projects the time and space to grow naturally at their own pace.

This approach is important because the year of the Tiger can be awkward for Snakes. For a start, you and the Tiger have very little to say to each other. You want very different things and don't really understand the other's point of view.

So, while the Tiger is not hostile to you, Snake, it doesn't go out of its way to be supportive either. There could even be an element of fear involved as the Tiger belongs to the Wood family of creatures and the Snake is a member of the Fire clan. Since Fire burns Wood – if it gets the chance – it wouldn't be surprising if the Tiger prefers to keep its distance.

On the other hand, if the Snake does manage to outsmart Tiger, that Wood could feed Snake's flames very usefully. So, sophisticated Snakes will make big gains in 2022 by stealth. You may not change jobs this year, Snake, but you will be rising up the ladder so smoothly no one will notice until you suddenly come out at the top.

The other challenge this year is 2022's Water element which does not suit Snake's Fire. Cash and emotions – enhanced by Water energy – are splashing around in the Serpent orbit, but without careful handling, there will be a lot of hissing and spluttering and nothing to show for it.

Yet Snakes have a genius for unobtrusive efficiency. The Snake finances will withstand any storms and still manage to benefit from the prosperous atmosphere.

Snakes involved in creative pursuits, particularly decorative arts, are set to do particularly well. Fashion, painting, ceramics, design – nimble-fingered Serpents could make a name for themselves with something beautiful created this year. By 2023, we could all be wearing a Snake design or hanging it on our wall.

The Snake home will flourish in 2022. Many Snakes will be enjoying new premises and this year will get the perfect opportunity to put their own unique stamp on the place. It's very likely you'll discover a whole new talent as you're inspired to experiment with some sort of craft or embellishment. Don't dismiss this gift as nothing more than a simple hobby. As your skill increases, you could find yourself with a whole new career next year.

Like most signs, opportunities for travel have been limited these last couple of years but, in 2022, the Snake holiday is back on course. If you're typical of your sign, you love to bask in the sun, Snake, and this year you'll have your chance. A far-flung beach looks like it's got your name on it in 2022, Snake, and a sunshine cruise could be in the offing too. Most Snakes will have done so well that several holidays could be a serious option for 2022.

Finally, many Snakes have recently found themselves further from their families or special friends than they'd like. 2022 is set to change all that. Ok, so you're unlikely to find yourselves living next door, but this is the year they'll find a way to come to you much more frequently. Start planning some of your elegantly enjoyable little parties – they're going to be needed!

What it Means to Be a Snake

Imagine, for a moment, a creature that was incredibly beautiful, wise, intelligent, graceful, sophisticated and respected. A creature always unhurried, yet attaining its goals, apparently without effort.

What would you call this amazing beast? Well if you were Chinese, you'd probably call it a Snake. That's right – a Snake.

Here, in the West, Snakes are almost as unwelcome as Rats and have been ever since Eve was persuaded to eat that apple in the Garden of Eden by a wily serpent. Most of us wouldn't have a good word to say for Snakes. Yet, in the East, it's a different story. There, all manner of positive qualities are discerned in the Snake, and the zodiac Snake is a good sign to be born under.

What's more, if we can forget all preconceived notions and look afresh at the much-maligned serpent, we have to admit there's something quite remarkable – almost magical – about the Snake.

For a start, Snakes don't have eyelids, which makes their stare particularly disconcerting. Astonishingly, they can shed their entire skins without ill effect, and slide away with a brand new, rejuvenated, wrinkle-free body – a feat many a human would envy.

Then there's the way they slither along without the need for legs – a bit repellent to a lot of people, but it can't be denied there's something uncanny about it. It's a surprisingly efficient means of locomotion too, and at times Snakes can move with astonishing speed. Quite a few of them can do this in water as well as on land, which makes them remarkably adaptable.

Snakes are in no way cuddly, but it seems even in the West we've retained a faint memory of a time when we recognised wisdom in the serpent. The Rod of Asclepius – the familiar symbol of a snake twisted around a pole – is still a widely used and recognised medical sign, seen outside pharmacies and doctors' surgeries, even if we don't know that Asclepius was the Greek God associated with healing. And in Greece, in the dim and distant past, snakes were sacred and believed to aid the sick.

The Chinese zodiac Snake is regarded as possibly the most beautiful of all the creatures, and people born under this sign somehow manage to present themselves in such an artful way, they give the illusion of beauty, even if not naturally endowed.

The Snake is physically graceful too. Each movement flowing into the next with effortless, elegant economy. Even when they're in a hurry, Snakes appear calm and unrushed, and should they arrive late for an appointment they're so charming and plausible with their excuses they're always forgiven.

This is a sign of great intelligence and subtlety. Snakes are never pushy, yet can usually slide into the heart of any situation they choose. Their clever conversation and easy charm makes them popular at any gathering. Yet, the Snake is picky. Snakes prefer to conserve their energy and don't waste it on activities and people of no interest to them. They are self-contained, quite happy with their own company if necessary, and seldom bored.

At work, Snakes are quietly ambitious, but in line with their policy of conserving energy wherever possible, they will aim for the quickest, easiest route to their goals. Just as the mythical Snake crossed the celestial river wrapped around the hoof of the Horse, the Snake is quite content to link their fortunes to those of a rising star so that Snake is carried to the top in their wake. Ever practical, the Snake has no need for an ego massage – the end result is what matters.

Other signs often mistake Snake's economy of action for laziness, but this is short-sighted. In fact, the Snake is so efficient and so clever that tasks are completed with great speed, leaving Snake with plenty of time to relax afterwards. What's more, in the same way that a Snake can shed its skin, people born under this sign are quite capable of suddenly walking out of a situation or way of life that no longer suits them, and reinventing themselves elsewhere without regret.

They tend to do this without warning, leaving their previous companions stunned. Only afterwards do people learn that the Snake has been inert and silently brooding for months. But it's no good imploring Snake to return. Snake's actions are swift and irrevocable.

The Snake home is a lovely place. Snakes have perfect taste. They like art, design, good lighting, and comfort. They're excellent hosts. They may not often entertain, unless they can delegate the chores, but when they do, they make it a stylish occasion to remember.

Snakes are known for their love of basking in the sun, and zodiac Snakes are no exception. Trips involving long hikes uphill in the pouring rain will not impress the Snake, but a smart sun-lounger by an infinity pool in a tropical paradise... well, that would be Snake's idea of heaven.

Best Jobs for Snake

Fashion Model

Psychologist

Pharmacist

Personal Shopper

Nail Technician

Designer

Astrologer

Perfect Partners

Cupid's arrow can strike anywhere at any time, of course, but once the novelty of new romance wears off, some relationships are easier to maintain than others. Here's a guide to the Snake's compatibility with other signs.

Snake with Snake

This fine looking couple turn heads wherever they go. Beautiful and perfectly dressed these two look like the perfect match. They never stop talking and enjoy the same interests so this could be a successful relationship. Long-term, however, there could be friction. They're both experts at getting what they want using the same sophisticated techniques, so they can see through each other.

Snake with Horse

At some level, perhaps, Horse remembers how Snake beat him in the calendar race, so despite an initial attraction, these two could be wary of each other. Snake is impressed by Horse's energy and athleticism while Horse admires Snake's elegance and charm. Yet they don't really have much in common. Deep thinking Snake could find Horse rather shallow and Horse may see Snake as frustratingly enigmatic.

Snake with Goat

Snake and Goat could enjoy many happy hours touring art galleries and exhibitions together. Neither of them craves excitement and harsh, adrenaline-boosting activities, and both appreciate creative artistic personalities. There's no pressure to compete with each other so these two would sail along quite contentedly. Not a passionate alliance but they could be happy.

Snake with Monkey

These two clever creatures ought to admire each other if only for their fine minds and, at first, it's possible they might. But unless they're really determined to make it work, it won't be long before active Monkey finds Snake's energy-saving ways irritating, while Snake loses patience with Monkey's endless jokes.

Snake with Rooster

Surprisingly, Snake and Rooster work well together. Both gorgeous in different ways, they complement each other without competing. Snake's keen eyes can see beneath Rooster's proud facade to the sensitive, unsure person inside, while Rooster appreciates Snake's unobtrusive strength and wise words of encouragement at just the right moment. These two could be inseparable.

Snake with Dog

Some snakes seem to have an almost hypnotic power and, for some reason, Dog is particularly susceptible to these skills. We've heard of snake-charmers, but snakes can be dog-charmers and, without even trying, Snakes can find themselves the recipients of Dog devotion. Since the Dog is strong, loyal, and can be fun, Snake is not averse to this but might, in the end, find it boring.

Snake with Pig

Pig and Snake don't have a lot to say to each other. Snake can't be bothered with Pig's endless shopping, and Pig is hurt by Snake's snobbish attitude. They both enjoy the good things in life so a luxury fling could briefly be fun – a shared spa break might be a good idea – but in the long-term, this relationship is probably not worth pursuing.

Snake with Rat

The Snake shares Rat's good taste and being elegant, sophisticated, and smart will delight Rat at first sight. These two get on very well on an intellectual level but perhaps are better as good friends rather than long-term partners. The Snake's love of basking in the sun for hours strikes Rat as lazy and dull, while Rat's need to rush around doing deals and meeting people seems pointless and wearying to Snake.

Snake with Ox

Like Ox, the Snake is quietly ambitious and not given to racing around unless it's absolutely necessary. Ox, on the other hand, respects Snake's clever brain and understated elegance. These two could quickly discover how beneficial an alliance between them would be. They're both happy to give the other space when required but also step in with support when needed. This could be a very successful match.

Snake with Tiger

Not the best of romances. These two are so fundamentally different that any initial attraction is unlikely to last. Snake likes to bask and soak up the sun while Tiger wants to explore and discover. Tiger takes in the big picture at a glance and is off to the next challenge while Snake likes to pause, delve beneath the surface, and consider matters. It wouldn't take long before these two annoy each other.

Snake with Rabbit

This subtle pair could make a good combination. They both understand the value of working behind the scenes and neither has any desire to wear themselves out on endless adventures. They share a love of art, fine things, and quiet pleasures and they both enjoy an orderly home. These two could settle down very happily together.

Snake with Dragon

Surprisingly, this couple gets along beautifully. Snake's elegant appearance and quick but subtle mind intrigues Dragon, while Snake admires Dragon's success and endless energy. Snake has no need to battle for the limelight and is quite happy to sit back and support Dragon's schemes from the comfort of a stylish sofa. Which is all the encouragement Dragon needs.

Snake Love 2022 Style

Many people are baffled by the number of Snakes that remain single. Sexy, sensuous, and enveloped in a magnetic appeal so strong it's almost hypnotic – Snake attracts eager partners just by standing still and sipping absently from a stylish glass. And that's the single Snake again this year.

Part of the secret is that Snake appears not to be interested in the undignified scramble to pair up unfolding all around. Which presents an irresistible challenge to half the other signs, of course, who can't help trying their luck. But the point is, Snake's attitude is not a façade. The single Snake means it.

Single Snake has high standards and will not lower them simply because they're unattached. If the perfect match comes along, Snake might consent to audition it for the role of partner, but success is not guaranteed.

Last year, most single Snakes were too busy changing their lives to bother overmuch with romance. This year is looking more promising. Single Snakes are as much in demand as ever, but now they're ready to take love more seriously. Things could get interesting.

Attached Snakes are in the mood for home-making and want to transform their nests and their partners to match. This might go down well with said partners but, on the other hand, it could cause friction. The Water element is heightening emotions all around, so stand by for some spectacular rows – followed by some memorable making up.

Secrets of Success in 2022

Doing well in 2022 should be a walk in the park for you, Snake. The qualities required for serpent success are gifts you possess in abundance. For a start, owing to the complicated relationship between the Snake and the Tiger, Snakes are best advised to keep a low profile at all times.

So what's not to like? You are the master of sliding under the radar and reaching your goal unnoticed. No problem for Snake; Tiger won't suspect a thing.

Then there's resisting the urge to rush around like everyone else. Once again, staying put, conserving energy, and waiting until the time is right is second nature to the Snake. By remaining quite still – and silently observing – you will advance twice as far as those other signs in such a hurry.

The most difficult bit for you, Snake, will be dealing with the sloppy, emotion-fuelled illogical behaviour of colleagues and authority figures this Water year. You always appear calm but – as only you know – inside it's often a different story. Keep your blood pressure down with meditation or mindfulness and you'll sail past the trouble-makers with ease.

Snake Year at a Glance

January – The Ox year is coming to an end, and you'll be sorry to see it go. You've done well, but now's your chance to celebrate.

February – Time to relax. Work commitments are beginning to build, but don't be guilted into taking on too much.

March – An intriguing person joins your circle. You have a lot in common. Where could it lead?

April – Authority figures are demanding, but one in particular appreciates your efforts. Keep smiling.

May – Imperceptibly, things have been getting better and better. Work is rewarding in more ways than one.

June – Someone is trying to persuade you to embark on a reckless venture. You're not keen. Be diplomatic.

July – An arty friend wants to team up. Business or pleasure? It could be both. Check out all the options.

August – If you haven't already been away, start booking. That suitcase won't pack itself.

September – A call for help could result in a long-term partnership. Not necessarily romance, but who knows?

October – A serious figure offers a promotion or a role in a new project. Think it over carefully. Is it really your thing?

November – Work is getting busy, but you're planning next month's festivities. You can't start shopping too early.

December – Too busy turning your home into a tasteful grotto to bother about money matters. Lock up that credit card and all will be well.

Lucky colours for 2022: Green, Pink, Silver

Lucky numbers for 2022: 6, 8

CHAPTER 6: THE HORSE

Horse Years

30 January 1930 – 16 February 1931

15 February 1942 – 4 February 1943

3 February 1954 – 23 January 1955

21 January 1966 – 8 February 1967

7 February 1978 – 27 January 1979

27 January 1990 – 14 February 1991

12 February 2002 – 31 January 2003

31 January 2014 – 18 February 2015

17 February 2026 – 5 February 2027

Natural Element: Fire

Will 2022 be a Golden Year for the Horse?

Crack open the champagne, Horse; this is the year you've been waiting for. In the lottery of life, 2022-style, you've just won the jackpot!

You knew things were on the up last year – after the dreadful equine days of 2020 – but 2021 will have nothing on 2022.

If you're typical of your sign, you will have been grinding your teeth in frustration at the endless stop-start lockdowns, travel bans, and social distancing that seem to have been going on forever. It's been enough to give the most relaxed of Horses claustrophobia.

Well, now here comes the Tiger to set you free – the most essential requirement for the liberty-loving Horse. One way or another, the restrictions on your movements will be lifted, and you'll be able to canter out into the world and show off your true magnificence.

The main reason for your good fortune, Horse, is that you and the Tiger are best buddies. The Tiger is particularly fond of Horses and will look on your adventures – even the more unwise notions – with indulgence.

You can afford to experiment a little and take a few risks in 2022, Horse because – chances are – you'll get away with them. Don't go crazy, of course, because even Tiger's pet equine can push things too far. Tweak the Tiger's tail, and the response will be terrifying.

Yet, within reason, everything you touch will seem blessed. Horses can look forward to promotion at work, increases in salary, and gratifying appreciation all around. Professional Horses will gain brilliant new contacts and enhance their reputations, while business Horses can expect to be showered with new contracts. Cash will follow all of these happy circumstances.

Many Horses will be inspired to study for additional qualifications in 2022 and, as long as they make an effort, they're likely to succeed.

This would be an excellent time to start your own business too, Horse, if any brainwaves occurred during lockdown. Again, don't mortgage everything you own, but if you're sensible, the Tiger will help you every step of the way. A project begun this year could take off in a delightful way and set you up for decades to come.

The Horse belongs to the Fire family of creatures, while the Tiger is a Wood animal. Normally, this makes for a slightly uneasy relationship since Wood is very helpful for Fire, yet Fire exhausts Wood as it consumes it. In this case, though, Tiger's affection for the Horse is so great, assistance is gladly given, and there's always support when needed.

In day-to-day life, this could take the form of helpful friends appearing at just the right moment, loan companies saying 'yes' where previously they said 'no', or badly needed bargains turning up out of the blue.

No year is completely perfect, of course, and any glitches in 2022 are likely to be centred on the areas affected by the Water element. This year is a Water year, while the Horse is a Fire creature and – of course – Fire and Water is not a good combination.

Water has the happy effect of growing bank balances and easing communication, but on encountering Fire it has a nasty knack of dowsing the flames and putting a stop to things just as they get going.

At times, Horses could find promising projects suddenly disintegrating for reasons that seem to make no sense. They could also find colleagues becoming unusually moody and difficult. In fact, at times under this influence, Horse, you might be the one becoming moody and difficult!

Yet, despite the odd hic-up, the protection of the Tiger will shield you throughout, and setbacks will be kept to a minimum.

One thing many Horses will have missed these last couple of years is the type of big gathering Horses adore. Herd creatures such as the Horse flourish best when surrounded by the entire clan at fairly regular intervals. It's not that you don't need your own space, you do – quite frequently – yet now and then, Horses benefit from a quick blast of the communal energy generated when you all get together. Well, in 2022, stand by to be energised! There are a number of big family and friend occasions coming up, plus multiple festival visits.

In fact, you have so much fun, many Horses will choose to carry on partying at some sort of big communal holiday.

It looks like this is a year to remember, Horse.

What it Means to Be a Horse

Sleek and graceful, as well as strong and swift, the Horse has always been an object of admiration and often longing. Young girls dream of having their own pony while many adults, on acquiring a pile of cash, often treat themselves to a racehorse or at least a share in one.

In China, the Horse is believed to be a symbol of freedom, and you've only got to see a picture of the famous white horses of the Camargue, exuberantly splashing through the marshes, to understand why.

People born in the year of the Horse exude a similar magnificence. They tend to be strong and athletic with broad shoulders and fine heads of thick hair. Where would the Horse be without its mane? Most Horses excel at sports, especially when young. They can run fast if they choose, but they will happily try any game until they find the one that suits them best.

Horses, being herd animals, are gregarious types and don't like to spend too long alone. They enjoying hanging out with a crowd, chatting and swapping gossip, and Horses of both sexes can lap up any amount of grooming. They love having their hair brushed and fussed over, their nails manicured; a facial or relaxing massage is usually welcome.

Yet, Horses are more complex than they first appear. The affable, easy-going charmer, delighting everyone at a party, can suddenly take offence at a casual remark or storm off in a huff over some tiny hitch almost unnoticeable to anyone else, leaving companions baffled. They tend to stay baffled too, because it's difficult to get a handle on what upsets the

Horse since what annoys them one week may leave them completely unruffled the next.

The trouble is, although they look tough, Horses are, in fact, very sensitive. Inside, they're still half-wild. Their senses are incredibly sharp, and although they don't realise it, deep down they're constantly scanning the horizon and sniffing the air for the first signs of danger. As a result, Horses live on their nerves. They tend to over-react when things don't go completely to plan, and have to work hard to control a sense of panic. Ideally, Horses would like to bolt away when the going gets rough but as this is not usually possible, they get moody and difficult instead.

Provide calm, congenial conditions for a Horse, however, and you couldn't wish for a friendlier companion. The Horse is lively, enthusiastic, versatile, and fun.

At work, the Horse wants to do well but can't stand being fenced in or forced to perform repetitive, routine tasks. Also, although they're good in a team, Horses have a need for privacy and independence so they may change jobs frequently until they find the right role. Yet, when they're happy, Horses will shine.

At home, Horse is probably planning the next trip. Horses like to be comfortable but they're not the most domesticated of the signs. They love being in the open air and don't see the point of spending too much time wallowing on a sofa or polishing dusty ornaments. They may well spend more time in the garden than indoors. On holiday, Horse loves to head for wide-open spaces – a vast beach, a craggy hillside or a mountain meadow; Horse would be thrilled to explore them all.

Best Jobs for Horse

Personal Trainer

Hairdresser

Vet

Golf/Tennis Coach

Jockey

PE Teacher

Dancer

Horse Whisperer

Perfect Partners

Cupid's arrow can strike anywhere at any time, of course, but once the novelty of new romance wears off, some relationships are easier to maintain than others. Here's a guide to the Horse's compatibility with other signs.

Horse with Horse

No doubt about it, these two make a magnificent couple, and any foals in the family would be spectacular. They certainly understand each other, particularly their shared need for both company and alone time so, in general, they get on well. The only tricky part could come if they both grew anxious over the same issue at the same time. Neither would find it easy to calm the other.

Horse with Goat

Goat and Horse just click! These two love kicking up their heels and trotting off into the green. Goat doesn't need to go far or do anything strenuous but is always up for a break in routine, while Horse doesn't do routine at all so is constantly on the lookout for a partner ready to escape. This couple rarely considers the consequences but, mostly, they don't need to.

Horse with Monkey

Uh oh – best not attempted unless it's love at first sight. Monkey and Horse have wildly different outlooks and can't seem to see eye to eye on anything. They're both lively but in different ways that don't complement each other. Monkey will consider Horse's moods illogical and pointless while Horse is irritated that Monkey makes no attempt to understand how Horse feels. Very hard work.

Horse with Rooster

The eye-catching Rooster intrigues Horse while Rooster appreciates Horse's strength and agility. They can enjoy many stimulating dates together. Yet, in the long-run, this couple may not be able to provide the stability the other needs. They're both sensitive types but in different ways. After a while, the relationship could run out of steam.

Horse with Dog

Both good friends of man, these two can make a formidable team. Dog understands the occasional need for solitude while admiring Horse's strength and agility. Horse, meanwhile, senses Dog's loyalty and down to earth nature. Both lovers of the great outdoors and physical activity, they'll never be short of adventures to share. A promising long-term relationship.

Horse with Pig

Pig and Horse are good companions. Horse is soothed by easy-going Pig and Pig is proud to be seen with such an alluring creature as Horse. They don't have a lot of interests in common, but they don't antagonise each other either. They can jog along amicably for quite a while, but long-term they may find they each want more than the other can provide.

Horse with Rat

Rat and Horse both fizz with energy, and they love action and looking good, yet this is not seen as an ideal partnership. Nothing's impossible of course, but these two will have to work hard to find harmony. The Rat will admire Horse's enthusiasm and cheerful approach but become impatient to discover Horse can also be fiery and emotional. Horse, on the other hand, can find Rat's risk-taking behaviour extremely worrying.

Horse with Ox

Long ago on many Western farms, Ox was replaced by the Horse, and it may be that Ox has never forgotten and never forgiven. At any rate, these two, despite both being big, strong animals are not usually friends. Horse is too flighty and frivolous to interest Ox for long, while Ox's methodical, careful ways will irritate the Horse. Best not to go there.

Horse with Tiger

This athletic pair gets on pretty well. They both like physical pursuits, testing their strength out of doors or just enjoying the feel of the wind in their hair and the ground under their feet. True, Horse may not quite understand Tiger's plans for world domination, but it doesn't really matter. Horse is happy to be loyal to such a charismatic partner. As they're both moody, there could be rows but making up is exciting.

Horse with Rabbit

This could be tricky. It's fairly unlikely that Horse and Rabbit would ever end up on a date, but if they did and there was a strong attraction, it could lead to a love/hate relationship. Rabbit's neat and tidy ways would enrage Horse and Horse's unpredictable moods and over-the-top reactions would annoy Rabbit. Soon, Horse is likely to bolt for the hills or Rabbit retreat to its burrow.

Horse with Dragon

The athletic Horse is pretty good at keeping up with dashing Dragon. And Dragon appreciates a partner who enjoys getting out and about as much as Dragon does. Yet Horse might grow weary of Dragon's constant new projects and resent having to be involved. Horse likes to go off and do Horsey things at frequent intervals which Dragon tends to view as disloyal. This relationship could get fiery.

Horse with Snake

At some level, perhaps Horse remembers how Snake beat him in the calendar race, so despite an initial attraction, these two could be wary of each other. Snake is impressed by Horse's energy and athleticism while Horse admires Snake's elegance and charm. Yet they don't really have much in common. Deep thinking Snake could find Horse rather shallow, and Horse may see Snake as frustratingly enigmatic.

Horse Love 2022 Style

How can you fail this year, Horse? Even at the worst of times, your sleek good looks and natural grace capture every glance in the room, but in 2022 – basking in the approving glow of the Tiger – you are truly radiant. No one can take their eyes off as you canter by and, next thing you know, they'll be begging to spend more time at your side.

Single Horses could even become a little arrogant after so many months in the admiring spotlight. You may find yourself getting more and more picky and dismissing prospective partners for the most minor of imperfections.

There's also that awkward Water element to contend with. Previously calm types could be rendered unexpectedly temperamental and annoying this year, and prone to misunderstanding what you say. Well, right now, the single Horse will tolerate no nonsense in romance. Looks like an exciting but turbulent 12 months.

Attached Horses may be deciding to head for pastures new with their beloved this year. That call of the herd is likely to sound particularly strong for settled Horses. The pair of you may soon be happily house-hunting to move closer to the extended family and old friends.

Secrets of Success in 2022

You're feeling lucky, Horse; ready to delve into all those exciting new ventures you once dismissed as daydreams. Quite right, too. You've got so much going for you this year it would be a crime not to make the most of all that potential.

Yet to maximise your chances of success, you do need to be a little cautious. Things are going so well there's a danger you could become overconfident or complacent. You're not the type to enjoy sitting around mulling over every tiny detail, Horse, and this energetic year is likely to make you more restless than ever. However, you could lose out big time by a slapdash approach to the small print. If you can't be bothered to do it yourself, Horse, hire someone trustworthy to handle the technical stuff.

Then there's the small matter of your spending, Horse – though 'small' is probably not the right term. Try 'large' or even 'extravagant'! This year, the cash is rolling in so merrily you feel more than justified in spraying it around like a Grand Prix driver on the winner's podium.

If you want your wealth to follow you into 2023, Horse, how about saving some of it or making some wise investments?

The Horse Year at a Glance

January – Excitement is bursting out all over. Things are good and getting better.

February – Belated celebrations are heading your way, and a Valentine has your name on it.

March – Spring is in the air, and you're feeling frisky. An early break beckons, plus a job interview.

April – The boss is considering you for higher things. You have your own plans, though. Is it possible to do both?

May – Compromises are the order of the day. You can have your cake and eat it if you come up with a clever solution.

June – A big get together is being planned, and clothes are on your mind. The right outfit is essential.

July – Summer is for being out of doors, but work keeps calling. A pay rise may help concentrate your mind.

August – All your projects are going well. You're in the mood to celebrate.

September – A new romance looks lively. It may not last, but you'll enjoy exploring.

October – A colleague or partner proves invaluable. Joint success is on the cards.

November – It looks like you're getting nagged over spending. You can afford a splurge, but could they have a point?

December – Time to plan a great big, family festivity. This year, you'll make your mark.

Lucky colours for 2022: Green, Silver, Purple

Lucky numbers for 2022: 8, 3, 1

CHAPTER 7: THE GOAT

Goat Years

17 February 1931 – 5 February 1932

5 February 1943 – 24 January 1944

24 January 1955 – 11 February 1956

9 February 1967 – 29 January 1968

28 January 1979 – 15 February 1980

15 February 1991 – 3 February 1992

1 February 2003 – 21 January 2004

19 February 2015 – 7 February 2016

6 February 2027 – 25 January 2028

Natural Element: Fire

Will 2022 be a Golden Year for the Goat?

Well, now Goat. This looks interesting. Are you in the mood for love? I hope so because 2022 seems to be weaving some very romantic velvety strands around the Goat homestead.

Even in your modest way, if you assume this can't apply to you – you could well end up with a big surprise.

When you think about it, if you're typical of your sign, you've probably spent the past year recuperating from the trials and tribulations of 2020.

No one would guess it from your cheerful exterior, but the Goat constitution, while physically strong, is incredibly sensitive. In fact, Goats are the silent worriers of the zodiac, inwardly chewing over every tiny problem or unkind word. Upheavals, unpleasantness, or dramas – both good and bad – play havoc with the Goat nerves.

This makes it very difficult for the Goat to get on with important tasks when any kind of turbulence is washing around. Goats need a tranquil atmosphere to reach their full potential.

So, it wouldn't be surprising, after the tensions and anxieties of the last couple of years, if many Goats are only just beginning to regain their equilibrium.

During the quieter energy of 2021, Goats began to start unwinding and can now enjoy the New Year almost fully restored. Just as well because the demanding Tiger has some treats in store – but Tiger treats tend to be on the boisterous side.

2022, for the Goat, is more about socialising, making new friends, and creating a beautiful haven, than about ambition and mercenary career gains. But this doesn't worry Goat one bit. In fact, this is just the way most Goats prefer life.

The truth is, the Tiger and the Goat – while respecting each other – don't really 'click'. The Tiger would like to see Goat happy but doesn't understand how this can be achieved, so sends along various harmonious helpers in the hope that something agreeable sticks.

This energy plays out in day-to-day life as a continuous stream of neighbours, colleagues, old friends, and long lost relatives turn up in the Goat orbit, eager to assist, team up, offer advice, or generally make Goat's life easier in any way they can.

If you're typical of your sign, Goat, you're a sociable type and will find this delightfully entertaining. Some very special invitations will emerge as a result, many of them connected with happy events – weddings, Christenings, graduation ceremonies, party celebrations – all are likely to be on the Goat itinerary this year. This means, of course, that you will have to treat yourself to a whole new wardrobe, or at least put the Goat creative skills to good use and make yourself a unique outfit.

Last year, many Goats will have been honing their artistic gifts and possibly beginning to build their own businesses in a craft field. Despite the fact that career is not emphasised this year, Goats in creative industries will do well without even trying especially hard. This is partly because Goats don't really think that using their artistic skills is 'work' and partly because the element this year is Water, and Water encourages the arts, media, and everything involved in communication.

By combining the good fortune associated with helpful friends with the luck beaming towards artistic pursuits, the Goat could accidentally end the year with a thriving and expanding business!

And even though most Goats are not plotting pay rises, the Water element also helps money flow, so at least one pleasing windfall is likely to swell the Goat coffers and possibly more.

Many Goats moved house last year, and 2022 is earmarked for putting their own quirky stamp on the new quarters. Renovating, repainting, and redesigning is a joy to most Goats, so many blissful months will be spent turning the Goat residence into the palace of their dreams.

Travel is also highlighted. Despite their pre-occupation, the typical Goat will allow themselves to be dragged away from home remodelling for a series of adventures, probably overseas. Here the possibility of romance is likely to unfold. So don't turn down any travel invitations. They could end up leading to a whole new future.

What it Means to Be a Goat

If people born under the sign of the Goat tend to look a little puzzled, uncertain even, who could blame them? It's not even definite their sign is the Goat. Some authorities call their sign the Sheep. Others – the more macho types – have it down as the Ram.

The confusion seems to stem from different translations of the original Chinese word.

But what's in a name? Whatever you call it, the qualities ascribed to the Goat/Sheep/Ram are the same. In China, the sign is regarded as symbolising peace and harmony. What's more, it's the eighth sign of the zodiac and the number eight is believed to be a very lucky number, associated as it is with growth and prosperity.

So, all you confused Goats out there can relax in the knowledge you were born in a lucky year.

In truth, perhaps the gentle sheep – the living animal that is – does resemble the zodiac Goat more than the real-life goat. Flesh and blood goats tend to have a feisty, combative quality and a strongly stubborn streak. Those sharp, pointy horns and all that head-butting does tend to put people off.

Yet, people born in a Goat year are known as the sweetest and friendliest of all the signs. They possess no spikey quality at all. They are tolerant and kind, have no wish to be competitive, and want to see the best in everyone they meet. Though they may not realise it, this attitude often unconsciously brings out the best in others, so the Goat's expectations are usually fulfilled.

Goats seem to get on with almost everyone, even people that others can't abide.

What's more, Goats usually possess a wonderful artistic talent. Even those Goats who feel they can't paint, draw, or manage anything skilled, are nevertheless immensely creative with a fine eye for colour and design.

The Goat loves beautiful things and even sees beauty in objects and places that hold no appeal for others. They love to use their hands in their spare time, ideally making something practical yet decorative. Knitting, card-making, cake-decorating, gardening, or renovating old furniture, even DIY, will give them great pleasure.

Concepts such as time and also money, have little meaning for the Goat. When the Goat gets lost in inspiration, hours pass in seconds and Goat ends up late for anything else that might have been on the agenda.

Similarly, money is frustrating for the Goat. Goats are not materialistic; neither are they particularly ambitious in a worldly way. Objects other people regard as status symbols hold little Goat appeal so they can't see the point of putting in a lot of energy to acquire them. For this reason, Goats are not career-driven. All they really want to do is pursue their artistic project or latest interest. If this won't provide an income though, they'll do their best at whatever job turns up, in order to get back to their true vocation at weekends.

The perfect scenario for the Goat would be a big win on the lottery, so they never have to waste time on a conventional job again. Should this ever happen, they'd be advised to get someone else to look after the funds for them; Goats are not good at handling finances, and the windfall could slip through their fingers with distressing speed.

Goats are notoriously impractical with matters such as bills, household repairs, filling in forms, and meeting deadlines. They just can't seem to find the time to tackle such mundane items. Though they're intelligent people, they'll frequently claim not to understand such things. The truth is, of course, the ultra-creative Goat brain just can't be bothered.

One thing Goats do have in common with the flesh and blood animal is their stubborn streak. Despite that easy-going, sunny nature, zodiac Goats can astonish their friends by suddenly digging in their heels over what looks to others like a trivial matter of very little importance. Once Goat has adopted this position, it will not budge, no matter how unreasonable or how poor the outcome is likely to be.

The Goat home is an intriguing place. Striking and original, it's likely to be filled with mismatched treasures Goat has picked up along the way. Goats love car boot sales, junk shops, and galleries. They enjoy beach-combing and collecting branches and broken wood on country walks. They've even been known to 'rescue' items from rubbish skips. Somehow, Goat manages to weave together the most unpromising items to create a pleasing effect.

Best Jobs for Goat

Garden Designer

Craft Teacher

Interior Designer

Ceramic Artist

Furniture Restorer

Travel Agent

Antiques Specialist

Perfect Partners

Cupid's arrow can strike anywhere at any time, of course, but once the novelty of new romance wears off, some relationships are easier to maintain than others. Here's a guide to the Goat's compatibility with other signs.

Goat with Goat

When things are going well, you won't find a happier couple than two Goats. They are perfectly in tune with each other's creative natures and understand when to do things together and when to step back and give the other space. And since they both share the same interests, their together times are always fun. Yet, when practical problems arise, neither can easily cope. With a helpful friend on speed-dial, this would work.

Goat with Monkey

Monkey and Goat are different but in a good way. Though they don't quite 'get' each other deep down, Goat admires Monkey's lively personality and magical ability to come up with solutions for everything, while curious Monkey enjoys Goat's knowledge of the arts and the unusual. Long-term, Goat might not present enough of a challenge for Monkey but, with effort, it's a promising match.

Goat with Rooster

Peaceful Goat is not one to make feathers fly, so these two are unlikely to fall out, but they're unlikely to find perfect compatibility either. Goat is unable to give Rooster the regular ego boosts that make Rooster thrive while Rooster is baffled by Goat's unpredictable devotion to impractical projects or people. Misunderstandings are likely.

Goat with Dog

This is another relationship that could be tricky. Loyal Dog would be quite willing to stand by Goat when practical problems loom but could end up irritated by Goat's inability to learn from previous mistakes and so keeps making them. Goat can't understand why Dog gets so bothered. With care, these two could learn to live together.

Goat with Pig

Happy-go-lucky Pig and laid-back Goat make a good pair. They hate to stir up trouble and always look for a peaceful solution to any challenge. Ideally, they'd avoid the challenge altogether. They could be very contented together as long as Pig's spending and Goat's inability to deal with finances doesn't get them into trouble.

Goat with Rat

The Rat is charmed by carefree Goat and fascinated by its artistic talent and happy knack of living in the present. Easy-going Goat tends to like everyone so is perfectly content to enjoy Rat's company. These two can get along fine, yet they don't really understand each other deep down. Long-term, the Rat may find Goat's lack of interest in the practical side of life irritating.

Goat with Ox

Though these two share artistic natures (even if in the case of the Ox, they're well hidden), deep down they don't 'get' one another. Ox may be beguiled at first by Goat's friendly, easy-going manner but then disappointed to discover Goat seems to find everyone equally delightful, even those who are plainly unworthy. Goat, on the other hand, can't understand why Ox won't lighten up more. This relationship would require a lot of effort and compromise.

Goat with Tiger

Tiger and Goat don't have a lot in common. While their aims and temperaments are quite different, they are both sociable creatures and Goat wouldn't mind Tiger attracting all the attention when they're out together. Tiger, in return, would appreciate Goat's lack of jealousy and generosity of spirit. Yet, long-term, they're likely to drift apart as they follow their different interests.

Goat with Rabbit

Wow! One glance across a crowded room and that's it for Goat and Rabbit. Rabbit instantly recognises and appreciates Goat's innate style and authenticity, while Goat admires Rabbit's restrained elegance and understated intellect. Both quiet, home-loving types, they also adore exploring and acquiring fine things. This couple will never be bored.

Goat with Dragon

Goat tends to baffle the busy Dragon. Dragon can see Goat is the creative type but can't understand why Goat doesn't appear to be working very hard when so much could be achieved. In fact, if they stayed together long enough, Dragon could help Goat make the most of many talents but it's unlikely either of them can sustain enough interest for this to happen.

Goat with Snake

Snake and Goat could enjoy many happy hours touring art galleries and exhibitions together. Neither of them craves excitement and harsh, adrenaline-boosting activities and both appreciate creative, artistic personalities. There's no pressure to compete with each other so these two would sail along quite contentedly. Not a passionate alliance but they could be happy.

Goat with Horse

Goat and Horse just click! These two love kicking up their heels and trotting off into the green. Goat doesn't need to go far or do anything strenuous but is always up for a break in routine, while Horse doesn't do routine at all so is constantly on the lookout for a partner ready to escape. This couple rarely considers the consequences, but mostly, they don't need to.

Goat Love 2022 Style

This is the year for romance for most Goats. Single, attached, or just not interested – makes no difference. The Tiger is out to brighten up your life with some welcome love interest.

Single Goats will be especially lucky. Goats have a wonderful style all their own. They don't dress for impact; they just throw together a colourful mix of all the looks that please their eye without a thought as to how it strikes anyone else. Yet, this very carefree, unselfconscious approach makes them stand out instantly in any crowd. So this year, single Goats are likely to be pleased, though a little perplexed, by all the attention coming their way. Everyone they meet seems to want more of the Goat charm and originality.

Expect a series of fun romances and possibly a holiday encounter that rapidly turns serious.

Attached Goats can look forward to just as much fun. Partners are appreciating you more than ever, and a series of romantic breaks and delightful date nights take your relationship to new heights. It could be that Fire and Water love/hate thing will spark a few heated arguments, but making up will make Goat's sparks fly.

Secrets of Success in 2022

Most Goats will probably be so focused on romance this year that they would be quite happy to put career matters on the back burner. Yet, although 2022 is not destined to be a big year for conventional ambition, the Goat can still find the kind of success that means most to them.

At heart, Goats are not materialistic. Goats love to climb, but to ever more interesting and stimulating heights. So, this year, the opportunities for creating the perfect Goat lifestyle just keep rolling in. Frequent socialising, apart from being fun, will result in new friends and valuable new contacts.

More time spent on those artistic hobbies, as well as being enjoyable, will result in creations that could have wide and surprisingly commercial appeal. Even cash will not be too much of a problem as the Water element keeps it flowing nicely.

The only pitfalls you should watch out for, Goat, are your knack of spending every penny that comes in and then a bit more (!), plus a tendency to say 'yes' to every offer and invitation. There are so many goodies coming your way now it's difficult to pick and choose, but the boisterous Tiger will wear you out if you're not careful. Pace yourself, tighten those purse strings, and you'll have the best year you've enjoyed for ages.

The Goat Year at a Glance

January – It might look gloomy outside, but an exciting project at home lifts your spirits.

February – An old friend reappears. This lively character gets you back out on the town again. Good times.

March – Some tempting new shops or online sites catch your eye. You love everything on offer! Don't go too crazy.

April – Work, what work? Seems like the boss is getting cranky. Time to look like you're slaving.

May – A colleague becomes your best buddy. The two of you make a brilliant team. Authority figures are pleased for a change.

June – Out and about in your spare time. You discover some intriguing new places. Inspiration strikes.

July – A surprise party or social event leads to romance. Take care not to spark jealousy.

August – A pay rise or unexpected bonus comes your way. Celebrate with a little holiday.

September – Goat ideas and artistic creations win applause. Colleagues are eager to help.

October – Home improvements are flourishing, but a gloomy neighbour is difficult to handle. Goat charm will soothe their temper.

November – Your career is going surprisingly well. Time to treat yourself to some well-deserved luxuries.

December – Everyone wants to come round to yours, Goat. It's party time, and you know how to party!

Lucky colours for 2022: Silver, Emerald, Terracotta

Lucky numbers for 2022: 9, 1, 3

CHAPTER 8: THE MONKEY

Monkey Years

6 February 1932 – 25 January 1933

25 January 1944 – 12 February 1945

12 February 1956 – 30 January 1957

30 January 1968 – 16 February 1969

16 February 1980 – 4 February 1981

4 February 1992 – 22 January 1993

22 January 2004 – 8 February 2005

8 February 2016 – 27 January 2017

26 January 2028 – 12 February 2029

Natural Element: Metal

Will 2022 be a Golden Year for the Monkey?

Ever fancied being a guru, Monkey, or a 21st-century agony aunt? Well, even if the idea never occurred to you before, you might find that in 2022 you've ended up becoming a combination of the two.

You didn't realise you'd become super-wise? Well, you will soon!

If you're typical of your sign, you'll have done pretty well last year as long as you managed to steer clear of the dreadful pandemic. Many Monkeys bought or sold property, or at least changed their address, cash wasn't too difficult to come by, and most of your projects worked out the way you wanted... eventually.

You begin 2022 in a good place. This is excellent because Tiger years are often more complicated for the Monkey. It's not that you can't flourish – it's just that you have to play your hand more carefully.

The reason is the Tiger is not a huge fan of the Monkey. You don't share the same cheeky sense of humour, and the Tiger doesn't approve of the Monkey's weakness for practical jokes.

In day-to-day life, this clash of personalities is likely to play out in the form of an irritating number of obstructive people crossing the Monkey path, and a frequent need to attend to tedious, apparently unimportant details. Everything that mercurial, quick-witted Monkey loathes.

Although the pace of the year is fast, these annoyances will slow your progress, Monkey, and make you cross.

Yet, since the Tiger is also a symbol of justice and fair play, if you can curb your talent for bending the rules and put in some serious effort, you will do well.

This is not the year for changing jobs or making bold investments. On the other hand, Monkeys that stay put and inject all their inventive, creative skills into their current role or project will reap huge rewards.

You also have the not so small matter of the elements to contend with. The Tiger belongs to the Wood family, while Monkey is a Metal creature. Traditionally, Wood is not too keen on Metal, associating it with axes, blades, and other cutting implements unfriendly to growing trees. Therefore, the Tiger will avoid the Monkey where possible. This energy might manifest this year in a number of Monkey brainwaves being ignored where normally they might be snapped up in delight, and Monkey projects getting mysteriously mislaid or lost.

This needn't be a problem. The clever Monkey will use 2022's vigorous energy of growth to beaver away behind the scenes, honing the ideas and projects to perfection, ready to unveil them next year to an amazed world.

Then there's the element of the individual year – Water in 2022 – in its strongest form. Metal and Water are believed to be excellent friends as far as Chinese tradition goes, but in a slightly uneven way. Metal is reckoned to nurture and support Water, so naturally Water enjoys having Metal around. While Metal gives this aid willingly, it is often exhausted by the effort. Think mother and demanding child, Monkey, and you get the picture.

Not long after the Tiger year sweeps in, many a Monkey will find their phone ringing endlessly with appeals for help, requests for professional advice or just a wise opinion on an awkward situation.

You may be called upon to mediate in domestic battles, champion friends and relatives in disputes with authorities, or untangle financial and medical complications on behalf of your nearest and dearest.

Something similar occurred last year, under the influence of the Water creature the Ox, but in a far milder form. You might as well regard what happened then as a kind of training, Monkey, because the same influence is back in 2022, only ten times as strong.

On the plus side, your efforts will – mostly – be greatly appreciated. In fact, after a while, you could be regarded as positively saintly. You could end up making quite a name for yourself as a sage, and your nuggets of wisdom spread far and wide. Who knows where this might lead in the future? Think your own radio show, podcast or even a book... everything's possible, Monkey.

What it Means to be a Monkey

There was a time when we tended to regard the Monkey as a figure of fun. The creature's awesome agility, effortless acrobatics, and natural clowning made us laugh, and if they sensed an audience, the animals would show off shamelessly. Which, of course, only made us enjoy them more.

Yet, in China, the Monkey was credited with far more qualities than merely those of a born entertainer. The sign of the Monkey is associated with intelligence, justice, and wisdom. Behind those mischievous eyes, the Chinese detected a shrewd brain and ability to plan the best course of action.

Like their namesakes, people born under the sign of Monkey tend to be physically agile. They're quick-moving, quick-thinking types with glittering wit and charismatic personalities. At a party, the Monkey will be in the centre of the group that's convulsed with laughter. Monkeys love jokes and humour of all kinds, and if anyone's going to start entertaining the crowd with a few magic tricks, it's likely to be a Monkey.

While not necessarily conventionally good-looking, the Monkey's lively face and sparkling eyes are always attractive, and Monkeys have no difficulty in acquiring partners. The tricky bit for a Monkey is staying around long enough to build a relationship.

People born under this sign need constant mental stimulation. They don't necessarily expect others to provide it. They are quite happy to amuse themselves with puzzles, conundrums, the mending of broken objects, and inventing things, but they also need new places and new faces. Few signs can keep up with Monkey's constant motion.

What's more, Monkeys are not good with rules or authority. They've seldom seen a rule that they don't want to break or avoid. In fact, it sometimes seems as if Monkey deliberately seeks out annoying regulations just for the fun of finding a way around them.

Yet, beneath the humour and games, the Monkey is ambitious with an astute brain. Monkeys can turn their hand to almost anything and make a success of it, but they're probably best-suited to working for themselves. If anyone is going to benefit from their efforts they believe it should be, chiefly, themselves. Also, they're not good at taking orders and, to be fair, they're so clever they don't need to. They can usually see the best way to carry out a task better than anyone else.

The Monkey home is often a work in progress. Monkey is always looking for a quicker, easier, cheaper, or more efficient way of doing everything and new ideas could encompass the entire building from the plumbing to the lighting and novel security systems. The first home in the street to be operated by remote control is likely to be the Monkey's. Yet, chances are, Monkey would prefer to meet friends in a nearby restaurant.

When it comes to holidays, Monkeys can have a bag packed seemingly in seconds, and are ready to be off anywhere, anytime. They don't much mind where they go as long as it's interesting, unusual, and offers plenty to be discovered. Lying on a sun-lounger for extended periods does not appeal.

Best Jobs for Monkey 2022

Manicurist

Acrobat

Chess Master

Inventor

Photojournalist

Repair Shop Expert

Party Entertainer

Perfect Partners

Cupid's arrow can strike anywhere at any time, of course, but once the novelty of new romance wears off, some relationships are easier to maintain than others. Here's a guide to the Monkey compatibility with other signs.

Monkey with Monkey

It's not always the case that opposites attract. More often, like attracts like and when two Monkeys get together, they find each other delightful. At last, they've met another brain as quick and agile as their own and a person who relishes practical jokes as much as they do. What's more, this is a partner that shares a constant need for change and novelty. Yet, despite this, two Monkeys can often end up competing with each other. As long as they can recognise this, and laugh about it, they'll be fine.

Monkey with Rooster

While not a perfect match, these two have got a lot of time for each other. Monkey recognises the intelligent brain beneath Rooster's plumage while Rooster admires Monkey's ability to entertain a crowd and they both adore socialising. They could enjoy many fun dates together. Long-term, though, Rooster may tire of Monkey's jokes.

Monkey with Dog

Monkey finds Dog intriguing. Monkey senses Dog's strength of character coupled with its playful streak, which fits well with Monkey's love of games. Dog, meanwhile, appreciates Monkey's energy and light-hearted approach. Yet, before long, Monkey's disdain for rules will grate on Dog's instinctive love of them. They cannot agree in this area, and it could lead to arguments.

Monkey with Pig

On the surface, these two might seem an unlikely couple. Yet Pig enjoys Monkey's fun and humour while Monkey is happy to be admired uncritically. What's more, Monkey's inventive mind can solve any difficulties caused by Pig's spending and since Monkey can't resist a challenge, the opportunity to retrain Pig, or at least find a way to obtain purchases cheaper, could help the relationship last.

Monkey with Rat

Unlikely as it might appear, mischievous Monkey and the clever Rat make a good partnership. Their quick minds, sociable natures, and love of novelty ensure that they're never bored together. True, Rat might sometimes feel that Monkey is too inclined to skim over the surface of things and could do with being more serious at times, but Monkey's ingenuity and audaciousness always saves the day. Both can have a weakness for gambling though, so need to take care.

Monkey with Ox

The naughty Monkey scandalises Ox but in such an amusing way that Ox can't help laughing. Monkey, on the other hand, is equally amused to find an audience so easy to shock. This unlikely pair enjoy each other's company and get on surprisingly well. Yet, right from the start, it's probably obvious to both that a long-term relationship couldn't last. A fun flirtation, though, could be a terrific tonic for them both.

Monkey with Tiger

Tiger can't help being intrigued by sparkling Monkey and Monkey is flattered by such interest. Who wouldn't enjoy being admired by such a fabulous creature? But irrepressible Monkey just can't help teasing, and being teased is not a sensation Tiger is familiar with (or appreciates). Unless the attraction is very strong, these two will wind each other up until they can bear it no longer and part.

Monkey with Rabbit

Mercurial Monkey doesn't really 'get' Rabbit. The Monkey can appreciate how well Rabbit operates and sees this approach gets good results, but it's all too picky and slow for Monkey. Rabbit, on the other hand, is amused by Monkey's quick wit and clever ways but deplores Monkey's slapdash, sometimes devious tactics. Very unlikely to work out.

Monkey with Dragon

These two are likely to hit it off immediately. Each is attracted to the other's intelligence and lively presence, and Dragon's exuberance doesn't overwhelm hyperactive Monkey. What's more, although they both enjoy being surrounded by a crowd, Monkey only wants to make people laugh while Dragon hopes to inspire them to a cause. There is no conflict, so this couple can help each other to go far.

Monkey with Snake

These two clever creatures ought to admire each other, if only for their fine minds and, at first, it's possible they might. But unless they're really determined to make it work, it won't be long before active Monkey finds Snake's energy-saving ways irritating, while Snake loses patience with Monkey's endless jokes.

Monkey with Horse

Uh oh – best not attempted unless it's love at first sight. Monkey and Horse have wildly different outlooks and can't seem to see eye to eye on anything. They're both lively but in different ways that don't complement each other. Monkey will consider Horse's moods illogical and pointless while Horse is irritated that Monkey makes no attempt to understand how Horse feels. Very hard work.

Monkey with Goat

Monkey and Goat are different but in a good way. Though they don't quite 'get' each other deep down, Goat admires Monkey's lively personality and magical ability to come up with solutions for everything, while curious Monkey enjoys Goat's knowledge of the arts and the unusual. Long-term, Goat might not present enough of a challenge for Monkey but, with effort, it's a promising match.

Monkey Love 2022 Style

Single Monkeys love to party, and in 2022 non-stop action will get the primate pulses racing. The Tiger energy surging around this year is fast, changeable, and bold – qualities that don't daunt Monkey one bit. There's nothing the single Monkey enjoys more than a challenge.

Right now, single Monkeys will be as desirable and sought after as ever, but there's an unexpected factor in the mix. A rival or competitor in love appears on the scene. If you couldn't make up your mind whether you were serious or not, Monkey, suddenly you are now.

Romance becomes much more exciting as you plot, plan, and devise any number of entertaining diversions to keep your love interested. You're bound to win in the end, Monkey, who could resist you after all? Just make sure though that when the game's over, you still appreciate your prize.

Attached Monkeys may find their partner needs much more TLC this year than usual. This is not necessarily the Monkey's forte, but after all the empathy and understanding you've been called upon to develop in other areas of life, it should be a doddle to practise a little more at home. It will be worth the effort. Monkey partners will be highly appreciative and may well shower their beloved with generous gifts and treats.

Secrets of Success in 2022

The great thing about being a near-genius, Monkey, is that you have the ability to turn almost any situation to your advantage. So this year, although the Tiger does not present you with the ideal environment in which to make your fortune, you're not fazed at all. Who needs ideal, after all, when solving a problem satisfactorily gives you so much of a buzz?

Right now, the trick is to expand your interests without drawing attention to your actions. Discretion and subtlety will work wonders. Let's face it, Monkey, you can be a bit excitable and over-ebullient at times. It's part of your endearing charm. Yet, this year, extrovert displays will annoy the Tiger. Keep a low profile, and quietly work your magic behind the scenes, and you will be amazed at the success you generate by the end of the year.

And even more than last year, take every opportunity to recharge your batteries. You are as energetic in your own way as the Tiger, but the constant pleas for help this year can be draining. Take a break whenever you get the chance, and you'll enjoy terrific gains by 2023.

The Monkey Year at a Glance

January – The last month of the Ox, and a final gift comes your way. Look back and admire how far you've come.

February – The Tiger year arrives to find you in a new home or greatly improved circumstances. Socialising increases.

March – A timid person needs your help. No problem for the versatile Monkey. You soon sort them out.

April – The boss is eyeing you up. In a good way or the opposite? They probably can't make you out. Explain things clearly.

May – You've had a cash building idea. And it will work, Monkey, but don't broadcast it far and wide.

June – An early holiday beckons. Despite appearances, you've been working hard. Take a break.

July – A love rival shows their face. No match for you, of course, but time to make more effort.

August – Nothing nicer than a summer party and you're having a ball. Watch out for sour expressions at work, though.

September – Jealous colleagues eye your work with envy. Ignore or pretend you don't notice.

October – A cash boost is heading your way. It could be a pay rise or some sort of win.

November – A romantic break somewhere luxurious is on the cards. No need to feel guilty.

December – Gifts galore in the Monkey household and festivities enjoyed at a different address.

Lucky colours for 2022: Tan, Gold, Pink

Lucky numbers for 2022: 8, 1, 5

CHAPTER 9: THE ROOSTER

Rooster Years

26 January 1933 – 13 February 1934

13 February 1945 – 1 February 1946

31 January 1957 – 17 February 1958

17 February 1969 – 5 February 1970

5 February 1981 – 24 January 1982

23 January 1993 – 9 February 1994

9 February 2005 – 28 January 2006

28 January 2017 – 15 February 2018

13 February 2029 – 2 February 2030

Natural Element: Metal

Will 2022 be a Golden Year for the Rooster?

Hi Rooster. Are you anywhere near a seatbelt? Well, if you are, you might like to fasten it now. You've got a bit of a roller-coaster year ahead – in a good way – but if you're not keen on roller-coasters, the coming months could be a touch unsettling.

If you're typical of your sign, Rooster, you'll have made good progress in 2021 but at a steady, sedate pace. Well, all that's about to change in 2022. Now the Tiger's muscled in – bristling with orange and black impatience – and determined to administer a metaphorical kick up the tail feathers to force you to spread those wings and fly.

This is going to turn out well for you, Rooster, but you won't necessarily enjoy the entire process.

Big changes were forecast for Roosters last year, and it's true many Roosters will begin 2022 in circumstances that have improved noticeably on the same period 12 months ago. Yet the Ox, ruler of 2021, is a slow-moving vehicle, and the incoming Tiger won't accept little more than a few well-sown seeds. The Tiger has total revolution in mind for the Rooster.

For a start, a radical overhaul of the Rooster budget will be demanded with a view to slashing overheads and dramatically increasing cash flow. Many Roosters will be changing jobs this year, and if you don't do it on your own initiative, Rooster, you might find yourself forced to make the break.

There's a brilliant new role waiting for you, but you've got to drag yourself out of your comfort zone to take advantage of it. Most Roosters will access the change through promotion or applying for tempting vacancies, but those that don't make the effort could find themselves the victims of company cutbacks and obliged to job hunt anyway. The Tiger will force you up the ladder one way or another!

Self-employed Roosters win the Tiger's approval, but there's still the feeling you could do far, far better. A big injection of extra energy and ingenuity will reap golden rewards this year, Rooster.

Then there's the Rooster home. If you're typical of your sign, you will have done pretty well financially last year, Rooster. But chances are you frittered away quite a chunk of the gains on flashy toys and fancy clothes.

The un-materialistic Tiger regards this as a waste. Tiger is not impressed by status symbols, so this year you're encouraged to put your cash to more serious use. Improving your home, moving somewhere better, or helping out good causes – especially those involved in the environment – will attract good luck.

Relationships get the same treatment. Any friends or lovers who are dragging you down will have to go, Rooster. Once again, if you don't begin the process of distancing yourself, the decision will be yanked out of your hands. Many Roosters will be baffled to find toxic 'friends' or so-called partners suddenly move away, stop getting in touch, or make themselves generally unavailable. This is not a cause for regret, Rooster, more a reason to celebrate. Replacements that will work out far better are on the way.

The reason for all this upheaval is the relationship between the Tiger and the Rooster. It's not that they don't get on, just that the Rooster tends to bring out Tiger's sense of frustration. The Tiger sees a great deal to admire in the Rooster, and much potential, but then gets irritated to find much of this latent talent goes untapped, partly due to Rooster's lack of confidence.

In a Tiger year, Tiger is determined to set Rooster on the right path, once and for all. And since this year it's the Black Water Tiger calling the shots, the Rooster who belongs to the Metal element, particularly favoured by Water, actually enjoys gentler Tiger treatment than usual.

So the good news, Rooster, is you may well end the year with a few ruffled feathers but richer, in a new home with a new partner, and a brand new circle of more agreeable friends.

What it Means to be a Rooster

Colourful, bold, and distinctly noisy, the Rooster rules the farmyard. Seemingly fearless and relishing the limelight, this bird may be small, but he doesn't appear to know it. We're looking at a giant personality here. This creature may be the bane of late sleepers, and only a fraction of the size of other animals on the farm, but the Rooster doesn't care. Rooster struts around, puffing out his tiny chest as if he owns the place.

The Chinese associate the Rooster with courage, and it's easy to see why. You'd have to be brave to square up to all-comers armed only with a modest beak, a couple of sharp claws, and a piercing shriek. Yet, Rooster is quite prepared to take on the challenge.

People born in the year of the Rooster tend to be gorgeous to look at, and like to dress flamboyantly. Even if their physique is not as slender as it could be, the Rooster is not going to hide it away in drab, black outfits. Roosters enjoy colour and style, and they dress to be noticed. These are not shy retiring types. They like attention, and they do whatever they can to get it.

Roosters are charming and popular with quick minds and engaging repartee. They have to guard against a tendency to boast, but this happens mainly when they sense a companion's interest is wandering. And since they're natural raconteurs, they can usually recapture attention and pass their stories off as good entertainment.

Like the feathered variety, Roosters can be impetuous and impulsive. They tend to rush into situations and commitments that are far too demanding, without a second thought and then, later on, wonder frantically how they're going to manage. Oddly enough, they usually make things work but only after ferocious effort. Roosters just can't help taking a risk.

Although they're gregarious and often surrounded by friends, there's a sense that – deep down – few people know the real Rooster. Underneath the bright plumage and cheerful banter, Rooster is quite private and a little vulnerable. Perhaps Roosters fear they'll disappear or get trampled on if they don't make enough noise. So they need frequent reassurance that they're liked and appreciated.

With all the emphasis Rooster puts on the splendid Rooster appearance, it's often overlooked that, in fact, the Rooster has a good brain and is quite a thinker. Roosters keep up with current affairs, they're shrewd with money and business matters, and though you never see them doing it, in private they're busily reading up on all the latest information on their particular field.

At work, Rooster wants to be the boss and often ends up that way. Failing that, Roosters will go it alone and start their own business. They're usually successful due to the Rooster's phenomenal hard work, but when things do go wrong, it's likely to be down to the Rooster's compulsion to take a risk or promise more than it's possible to deliver. Also, while being sensitive to criticism, themselves, Roosters can be extremely frank in putting across their views to others. They may pride themselves on their plain-speaking, but it may not do them any favours with customers and employees.

Rooster thinks the home should be a reflection of its owner's splendid image so, if at all possible, it will be lavish, smart, and full of enviable items. They have good taste, in a colourful way, and don't mind spending money on impressive pieces. If the Rooster can be persuaded to take a holiday, a five-star hotel in a prestigious location with plenty of socialising would be ideal, or a luxury cruise with a place at the Captain's Table.

Best Jobs for Rooster 2022

Demonstrator

Driving Instructor

Hotel Manager

School Head

TV Presenter

Perfect Partners

Cupid's arrow can strike anywhere at any time, of course, but once the novelty of new romance wears off, some relationships are easier to maintain than others. Here's a guide to the Rooster's compatibility with other signs.

Rooster with Rooster

Fabulous to look at though they would be, these two alpha creatures would find it difficult to share the limelight. They can't help admiring each other at first sight, but since both needs to be the boss, there could be endless squabbles for dominance. What's more, neither would be able to give the other the regular reassurance they need. Probably not worth attempting.

Rooster with Dog

Rooster and Dog are not the best of partners. Dog can be as plain-spoken as Rooster and is not likely to be impressed by overt show. What's more, Dog is often critical, and Rooster can't stand criticism. Rooster, on the other hand, is likely to sense and resent Dog's attitude. Frustration abounds for both in this relationship. Only for the hopelessly love-struck.

Rooster with Pig

These two might seem an unlikely couple – modest Pig with extrovert Rooster. Yet Pig has no need or wish to crow and can see the vulnerable character that lurks beneath Rooster's fine feathers; Rooster, meanwhile, responds to Pig's kindness and undemanding nature. As long as Rooster doesn't get bored, this can be a contented relationship.

Rooster with Rat

The first thing Rat notices about the Rooster is its beautiful plumage, but this is a relationship which is unlikely to get much further than initial admiration. Rooster's direct and frank approach can strike the Rat as tactless, while the Rooster can't understand why Rat has to make life so convoluted and complicated. Then again, Rooster's natural confidence and aplomb can come across as bragging to the Rat. These two have to be very determined to make a partnership work.

Rooster with Ox

For all its bravado and showing off, the Rooster is a down-to-earth type, drawn to security and accumulating the good things in life – requirements that Ox understands very well and can supply effortlessly. What's more, Ox can't help but admire Rooster's fine feathers and skill at communicating in a crowd – attributes Ox doesn't have and is unlikely to acquire. These two could enjoy a very good partnership.

Rooster with Tiger

The only feathered creature in the zodiac, the opulence and novelty of Rooster's appearance will draw Tiger like a magnet. What's more, deep down they are both quite serious-minded types so on one level they'll have much to share. Yet, despite this, they're not really on the same wavelength and misunderstandings will keep recurring. Could be hard work.

Rooster with Rabbit

A difficult match. However unfair it seems, Rooster comes over as loud, boastful, and uncouth to Rabbit while Rabbit appears dull, staid, and insufficiently admiring of Rooster's fine feathers to appeal to Rooster. These two just can't see below the surface of the other and it would be surprising if they ended up together. Only to be considered by the very determined.

Rooster with Dragon

A Dragon and Rooster pairing will always attract attention. These two are both gorgeous beings and love to be surrounded by admirers. They will probably enjoy going out together and being seen as a couple, but in the long-term they may not be able to provide the kind of support each secretly needs. Entertaining for a while but probably not a lasting relationship.

Rooster with Snake

Surprisingly, Snake and Rooster work well together. Both gorgeous in different ways, they complement each other without competing. Snake's keen eyes can see beneath Rooster's proud facade to the sensitive, unsure person inside, while Rooster appreciates Snake's unobtrusive strength and wise words of encouragement at just the right moment. These two could be inseparable.

Rooster with Horse

The eye-catching Rooster intrigues Horse while Rooster appreciates Horse's strength and agility. They can enjoy many stimulating dates together. Yet, in the long-run, this couple may not be able to provide the stability the other needs. They're both sensitive types but in different ways. After a while, the relationship could run out of steam.

Rooster with Goat

Peaceful Goat is not one to make feathers fly, so these two are unlikely to fall out, but they're unlikely to find perfect compatibility either. Goat is unable to give Rooster the regular ego boosts that make Rooster thrive while Rooster is baffled by Goat's unpredictable devotion to impractical projects or people. Misunderstandings are likely.

Rooster with Monkey

While not a perfect match, these two have got a lot of time for each other. Monkey recognises the intelligent brain beneath Rooster's plumage while Rooster admires Monkey's ability to entertain a crowd and they both adore socialising. They could enjoy many fun dates together. Long-term, though, Rooster may tire of Monkey's jokes.

Rooster Love 2022 Style

You have to admit Roosters have a certain reputation where romance is concerned. Like your unassuming cousin, the Rabbit, people tend to believe you're not exactly picky when it comes to partners. Maybe it's something to do with your splendid looks, colourful clothes, and the way you take such obvious pride in showing them off, but onlookers make the mistake of thinking this display is all about attracting new lovers.

They couldn't be more wrong. They fail to see the Rooster loves dressing up just for the sheer fun of it, and they're actually far happier settling down with one appreciative partner than wearing themselves out with a string of lovers.

Well, in 2022, you'll strut your stuff as magnificently as ever, Rooster, but as the months go on, you'll find yourself in unfamiliar settings. New friends will introduce you to a completely different circle, and you could end up discovering your soulmate amongst those fresh faces. Enjoy.

Attached Roosters need to have a serious think about their relationship. Are the two of you really happy? Are you both on the same page? Some Roosters might find the relationship has run its course and decide to part. Others will realise they've been taking their partner for granted and resolve to make amends, even if they don't say it out loud. After all, actions speak louder than words. Time for a second honeymoon?

Secrets of Success in 2022

Top of the list – take your fingers out of your ears, open your eyes, and come out from behind the sofa, Rooster! All you have to do to grasp the success of your dreams is to throw yourself into the action.

If you're typical of your sign, Rooster, you talk a good talk, you scrub up well (so you certainly look the part), yet few people realise that under that occasionally swaggering exterior, your confidence is as fragile as the most delicate porcelain. You're easily deterred and the brash energy of 2022 could send you scurrying to the sidelines to avoid the embarrassment of trying something that fails.

Well, puff out that chest, take a deep breath, and go for it, Rooster. For a start, the chances are it won't fail and secondly, you've got to be in it to win it. Shake off those doubts, give every promising opportunity your best shot, and you'll be amazed at what happens next.

The Rooster Year at a Glance

January – You've done pretty well so far, Rooster. The sales are on, the shops are full of tempting goodies… treat yourself. You deserve it.

February – Energy is running a little low this month. Keep out of the cold and stay by the fire to plot your next move.

March – A dreary person at work tries to pour cold water over your input. Try to ignore them – they're jealous.

April – Things are looking up. A new boss or authority figure is impressed. Keep on saying the right things.

May – Tempting offers abound. A promotion or work opportunity arrives, and romance is looking exciting.

June – You could have a choice between two prospective partners. Decisions, decisions! Try not to offend anyone.

July – An old friend reappears, and a trip away is in the offing. Things may not be quite the same, though.

August – House hunting could be on your mind. Don't rush into anything.

September – An extrovert character offers you a proposition. It could work well if the two of you don't clash. Think carefully.

October – Certain people in your orbit are being difficult. They may have problems. Be understanding.

November – Plans are shaping up well. Your career is improving and a cash boost arrives. Christmas is coming early.

December – Don't let family bickering spoil your fun. Celebrate with your wider circle for a carefree holiday.

Lucky colours for 2022: Yellow, Gold, Aqua

Lucky numbers for 2022: 2, 9

CHAPTER 10: THE DOG

Dog Years

14 February 1934 – 3 February 1935

2 February 1946 – 21 January 1947

18 February 1958 – 7 February 1959

6 February 1970 – 26 January 1971

25 January 1982 – 12 February 1983

10 February 1994 – 30 January 1995

29 January 2006 – 17 February 2007

16 February 2018 – 4 February 2019

Natural Element: Metal

Will 2022 be a Golden Year for the Dog?

Good news, Dog. In the lottery of the Year of the Tiger, you've just won joint-first prize! The Tiger just adores the devoted Dog, almost as much as the beloved Horse, and so – in 2022 – the two of you are destined to get first pick of all the favours on offer.

If you're typical of your sign, last year will have been an improvement on 2020, but there were still some tricky moments. As one of the born worriers of the zodiac, you can sniff out a cause for vague anxiety a mile off. The fact the problems often evaporate before they even reach the Dog orbit makes no difference. After all, next time, they might!

Fortunately, this year the Tiger energy is stronger and more defined than the type swirling around 2021's Ox, which suits the Dog much better. You like to know where you stand. Hints and subtle allusions leave you confused and irritated, and the Tiger understands and agrees with this attitude. So, in 2022, your choices will be more clear cut and you'll encounter people who say what they think, and do what they say – a greatly refreshing change.

Anyone who has been keeping secrets from you, Dog, or been less than honest will be found out this year. In fact, one particular piece of treachery might come as a shock. Yet don't regard the unmasking of this deception as a misfortune; it's a stroke of good luck that you've found out now.

Many Dogs have been thinking about moving house, and this year the perfect property is likely to come along. It might take longer than anticipated to get all the arrangements in place but don't worry, Dog, all will be well.

Yet, although quite a few Dogs may be considering changing jobs, as well as their home, this year, it might be better to stay put. Good luck is with you in all your projects, yet in 2022 it's probably wise to limit yourself to a few major alterations rather than tackle everything at once.

The reason for this is that the element of 2022 is Water, and the Dog is regarded as belonging to the Metal family of creatures. Water and Metal get along fine, but Metal is traditionally believed to support Water. In day-to-day life, this could play out as non-stop demands on Dog's time and energy.

Since Tiger is assisting you at every turn, Dog, these demands will probably be fun and entertaining, and you won't feel aggrieved. Yet even though you're strong and healthy, you're not Superdog. Pace yourself and make sure you allow plenty of time to relax.

Remaining in your current career looks like being a terrific decision too, as your loyalty could earn you an unexpected bonus this year. Self-employed Dogs need only carry on doing what they do so well to find their reputations and earnings enhanced.

Perhaps the biggest news of 2022 will surround family matters – which is why many Dogs will prefer not to get too busy at work. Suddenly, it seems as if each member of the Dog clan is making waves in their own individual way.

One temperamental type could suffer some sort of meltdown and need Dog's calming, sensible presence to soothe the storm. Another looks like running into financial difficulties while a third could be talking weddings and babies.

Since the Dog, almost more than any other sign, is extremely family-oriented, being on hand to untangle the twisty domestic knots is of the utmost importance. Few Dogs can sleep at night if their nearest and dearest are troubled.

Sorting it out will take time, Dog, but you'll save the day as you usually do and – deep down, you must admit – you love doing it. Finally, it looks like there's a memorable wedding in the offing, and you'll be playing some sort of starring role, Dog!

What it Means to be a Dog

Though some cultures are quite rude about the dog, and regard the very name as a disparaging term, in the West, we tend to be rather sentimental about our canine friends.

The Chinese, on the other hand, while regarding the zodiac Dog with respect, discern more weighty qualities in the faithful hound. They regard the sign of the Dog as representing justice and compassion. People born under the sign of the Dog, therefore, are admired for their noble natures and fair-minded attitudes.

Typical Dogs will do the right thing, even if it means they'll lose out personally. They have an inbuilt code of honour that they hate to break.

The Dog is probably the most honest sign of the zodiac. People instinctively trust the Dog even if they don't always agree with Dog's opinions. Yet Dogs are usually completely unaware of the high esteem in which they're held, because they believe they're only acting naturally; doing what anyone else would do in the circumstances.

Since they have such a highly-developed sense of right and wrong, Dogs understand the importance of rules. Also, since deep down they're always part of a pack – even if it's invisible – Dogs know that fairness is vital. If there aren't fair shares all round, there's likely to be trouble they believe. So, to keep the peace, Dog knows that a stout framework of rules is required and once set up, everyone should stick to them. Dogs are genuinely puzzled that other signs can't seem to grasp this simple truth!

People born under this sign tend to be physically strong with thick, glossy hair, and open, friendly faces. Their warm manner attracts new acquaintances, but they tend to stay acquaintances for quite a while. It takes a long time for Dog to promote a person from acquaintance to real friend. This is because Dogs are one hundred percent loyal and will never let a friend down, so they don't give their trust lightly.

Dogs are intelligent and brave, and once they've made up their mind, they stick to it. They're quite prepared to go out on a limb for a good cause if necessary, but they don't really like being alone. They're much happier in a group, with close friends or family. What's more, though they're good managers, they're not interested in being in overall charge. They'd much rather help someone else achieve a goal than take all the responsibility themselves.

At work, Dog can be a puzzle to the boss. Though capable of immense effort, and obviously the dedicated type, it's difficult to enthuse the Dog. Promises of pay rises and promotion have little effect. The Dog is just not materialistic or particularly ambitious in the conventional sense. Yet, if a crisis appears, if someone's in trouble or disaster threatens, the Dog is suddenly energised and springs into action. In fact, it's quite difficult to hold Dog back. Dogs will work tirelessly, without rest or thought of reward, until the rescue is achieved.

Bearing this in mind, Dogs would do well to consider a career that offers some kind of humanitarian service. This is their best chance of feeling truly fulfilled and happy at work.

At home, Dogs have a down to earth approach. Home and stability are very important to them. They're not the types to keep moving and trading up, but at the same time, they don't need their home to be a showcase. The Dog residence will be comfortable rather than stylish with the emphasis on practicality. Yet, it will have a warm, inviting atmosphere, and the favoured visitors permitted to join the family there will be certain of a friendly welcome.

It's not easy to get Dog to take a break if there's a cause to be pursued, but when Dogs finally allow themselves to come off-duty, they love to play. They like to be out in the open air or splashing through water, and can discover their competitive streak when it comes to team games.

Best Jobs for Dog

Army Officer

Police Dog Handler

Bank Clerk

Doctor

Ambulance Driver

Vet

Hotel Manager

Lifeguard

Perfect Partners

Cupid's arrow can strike anywhere at any time, of course, but once the novelty of new romance wears off, some relationships are easier to maintain than others. Here's a guide to the Dog compatibility with other signs.

Dog with Dog

Dogs love company so these two will gravitate to each other and stay there. Both loyal, faithful types, neither need worry the other will stray. They'll appreciate their mutual respect for doing things properly and their shared love of a stable, caring home. This relationship is likely to last and last. The only slight hitch could occur if, over time, the romance dwindles and Dog and Dog become more like good friends than lovers.

Dog with Pig

In the outside world, the Dog and the Pig can get along well together; in fact, Pigs being intelligent creatures can do many of the things dogs can do, so it's not surprising this zodiac pair make a good couple. Good-natured Pig is uncomplicated and fair-minded which suits Dog perfectly. Also, Pig brings out Dog's playful side – which delights Pig who's always keen to have a playmate. A happy relationship involving many restaurants.

Dog with Rat

The Rat and the Dog get along pretty well together. Both strong characters, they respect each other and give each other space when required. But deep down, the Dog is a worrier and gets anxious about unnecessary risks, while Rat just can't help sailing close to the wind if an interesting opportunity presents itself. Long-term, reckless Rat might unintentionally drive Dog to distraction. Only to be considered by Dogs with nerves of steel.

Dog with Ox

These two ought to get along well as they're both sensible, down to earth, loyal, and hardworking, and in tune with each other's basic beliefs. And yet, somehow they don't. Dog has a playful streak and finds this lacking in Ox, while Ox may be baffled by what seems like pointless silliness in Dog. If they can agree to differ, they could make a relationship work.

Dog with Tiger

While not exactly opposites, these two are different enough to intrigue each other yet similar enough in basic outlook to get on well. Both Tiger and Dog are idealistic and uninterested in material gain yet where Dog can be nervous, Tiger's bold. And where Tiger attracts controversy, Dog will be loyal. This partnership could be lasting and valuable.

Dog with Rabbit

Despite the fact that in the outside world Rabbit could easily end up as Dog's dinner, the astrological pair gets on surprisingly well. Dog appreciates Rabbit's careful, efficient ways and soft voice, while Rabbit admires Dog's energy and good intentions. Dog's lack of interest in the finer points of interior design might try Rabbit's patience, but with a little work, these two could reach an understanding.

Dog with Dragon

Not the easiest of combinations. Down-to-earth Dog can't see what all the fuss is about when it comes to Dragons. Unimpressed by glamour and irritated by what seems to Dog the gullibility of Dragon admirers, Dog can't be bothered to find out more. Dragon meanwhile, is hurt by Dog's lack of interest. Great determination would be needed to make this work.

Dog with Snake

Some snakes seem to have an almost hypnotic power, and for some reason, Dog is particularly susceptible to these skills. We've heard of snake-charmers, but snakes can be dog-charmers, and without even trying, Snakes can find themselves the recipients of Dog devotion. Since the Dog is strong, loyal, and can be fun, Snake is not averse to this but might, in the end, find it boring.

Dog with Horse

Both good friends of man, these two can make a formidable team. Dog understands the occasional need for solitude while admiring Horse's strength and agility. Horse, meanwhile, senses Dog's loyalty and down to earth nature. Both lovers of the great outdoors and physical activity, they'll never be short of adventures to share. A promising long-term relationship.

Dog with Goat

This is another relationship that could be tricky. Loyal Dog would be quite willing to stand by Goat when practical problems loom but could end up irritated by Goat's inability to learn from previous mistakes and so keeps making them. Goat can't understand why Dog gets so bothered. With care, these two could learn to live together.

Dog with Monkey

Monkey finds Dog intriguing. Monkey senses Dog's strength of character coupled with its playful streak, which fits well with Monkey's love of games. Dog, meanwhile, appreciates Monkey's energy and light-hearted approach. Yet before long, Monkey's disdain for rules will grate on Dog's instinctive love of them. They cannot agree in this area, and it could lead to arguments.

Dog with Rooster

Rooster and Dog are not the best of partners. Dog can be as plain-spoken as Rooster and is not likely to be impressed by overt show. What's more, Dog is often critical, and Rooster can't stand criticism. Rooster, on the other hand, is likely to sense and resent Dog's attitude. Frustration abounds for both in this relationship. Only for the hopelessly love-struck.

Dog Love 2022 Style

This is a terrific year for love, Dog. As the Tiger sets about improving the world, the ever-vigilant canine can finally relax, leave the heavy lifting to someone else, and turn their attention to lighter matters.

Single Dogs are in the mood to frolic and the other signs, sensing you're ready to play, will be queueing up for some fun and games. At times, Dog, you can come over a bit dour and serious – that's when you feel weighed down by responsibilities. But in 2022, the pressure eases and it's like you've been let off the lead.

Single Dogs rediscover their inner puppy – and you know how appealing a cute little puppy can be. Suddenly, prospective partners – who previously passed you by as too much of a challenge – are back for a second look, and chances are, they like what they see.

By the time the Tiger heads off for pastures new, the single Dog might be single no longer.

Attached Dogs will enjoy a fabulous year with their partner, as long as the partner is just as devoted to the family as they are. Most Dogs like nothing more than being surrounded by the rest of the pack and in 2022 family matters come into focus as never before. This could be a huge source of shared joy. If not, you might consider changing partners, Dog.

Secrets of Success in 2022

Once again, Dog, it looks as if success in the sense of 'climbing ever higher up the ladder' is not your top priority in 2022. Last year, many Dogs were sorting out the structural framework of their lives – by making alterations to the home or maybe moving altogether. This year they'll be too busy untangling the complicated personalities around them to be interested overmuch in work.

Yet, oddly enough, since your very good friend the Tiger is in charge, you need to exert yourself very little to do well. So even if you're not too bothered, Dog, it would be a good idea to carry on in your usual conscientious way. There's no need to take work home or put in extra hours over the weekend. Just by attending to the basics and keeping things ticking over, your career will gather momentum all by itself.

It might be tempting at times, when family dramas explode, to consider giving it all up for a quieter life, particularly as money will not be a problem. Yet, this would be a mistake. In the coming years, your career will seem more important, and you'll be very glad of the success you chalked up with ease in 2022.

The Dog Year at a Glance

January – You're in fine form and looking forward to the next 12 months. So many projects are on the go you hardly know where to start.

February – A great friend from the past reappears. Celebrations all around. You might have a house guest for a while.

March – Social stars are shining bright. It looks like you're flavour of the month. Romance arrives at a party.

April – Work's ticking over, but someone in your inner circle throws a moody. This has been brewing for a long time. Great patience is required.

May – An authority figure you admire is full of praise. Accept kind words gracefully, even if you're not sure you deserve them.

June – An exciting announcement in the family circle. It looks like another celebration is in order.

July – Someone's being picky at work. You're probably too busy to care.

August – A big holiday get-together brings good fortune. You could enjoy more than one. Take care that no one feels left out.

September – Someone has not been entirely straight with you; a deception comes to light. Deep down, you suspected all along.

October. One of your besties has had a windfall and wants to enjoy it with you. What's not to like!

November – Someone in the family is having problems with finances. Looks like Dog to the rescue.

December – The boss has a nice surprise for you and it looks like big festivities are planned chez Dog. Workmates might join the party too. Enjoy!

Lucky colours for 2022: Purple, Gold, Peach

Lucky numbers for 2022: 1, 3, 6

CHAPTER 11: THE PIG

Pig Years

4 February 1935 – 23 January 1936

22 January 1947 – 9 February 1948

8 February 1959 – 27 January 1960

27 January 1971 – 14 February 1972

13 February 1983 – 1 February 1984

31 January 1995 – 18 February 1996

18 February 2007 – 6 February 2008

5 February 2019 – 24 January 2020

Natural Element: Water

Will 2022 be a Golden Year for the Pig?

If you're typical of your sign, Pig, you're probably still wearing your party hat and haven't quite got around to hoovering the crumbs off the carpet yet, let alone tackled the washing-up.

Well, no worries, Pig. The Black Tiger is very fond of his little friend with the trotters; minor imperfections will be overlooked, and 2022 is destined to be an excellent year for you.

The curious thing about the zodiac Pig, is that while it might lack the obvious glamour of some of the more dramatic signs, it has a happy knack of rarely antagonising any of them. This means that, across most years, the Pig tends to sail through choppy conditions relatively unscathed.

In 2022, ruled by the friendly Tiger, you'll do much more than escape relatively unscathed, Pig. You're set to enjoy some exciting times and make a long-held dream come true.

There are many reasons for your good fortune. For a start, the Tiger belongs to the Wood family of creatures, while the Pig is regarded as a Water animal.

Since Wood – the element that represents plants – requires Water to grow, you're always welcome in Tiger's orbit, Pig. What's more, as one of the quieter signs of the zodiac, the dominant Tiger feels no compulsion to compete and is quite content to let Pig potter about doing Piggish things without interference.

For this reason, your ideas, innovations, and input will be welcomed at any meeting this year, Pig, and you'll find most people agree with whatever you have to say.

What's more, though Water signs are often called upon to help the Wood family should trouble arise, the Tiger is very protective of the Pig, and the opposite tends to apply. As a result, any situation likely to turn unpleasant for you this year will be quickly diffused.

In day-to-day life, this energy could take the form of helpful people turning up to aid the Pig at just the right moment, traffic lights turning suddenly green when Pig's in a hurry, or unwise emails getting accidentally deleted before the recipient can read them.

The other lucky aspect for the Pig is the fact that the element of 2022 is Water. Since the Pig is a Water animal, you'll feel completely in tune with the mood of the moment – you'll instinctively do the right thing – at the right moment – and will seldom say anything tactless, because this year you 'just know' what to do.

Water is believed to aid communication and also helps cash to flow, so 2022 is likely to wash new friends, new opportunities, and new sources of income into the Pig's orbit. Obviously, if you don't grab them before they float by, they could get washed out again, Pig, but most Pigs know a tasty goodie when they see one and won't be slow.

The emphasis on communication will also come into play as regards that long-held dream, Pig. Whether it involves a job or role you've always longed for, a romance, or maybe the holiday of a lifetime – your wishes will finally be understood in the relevant quarters, and the luck of the Tiger will ensure a way is found to grant them.

At work, the Pig talents are recognised, and a promotion looks likely. Business Pigs will have new customers flocking to their door, and self-employed Pigs could become famous for their skills. Many Pigs will even consider starting something completely different this year. As long as you've done the proper research, Pig, this is a good time to go for it.

Finances are usually a tricky subject for the typical Pig. The Pig likes to spend – or rather, to buy – and gets easily carried away with stacks of 'must-have' bargains. This generally results in even well-paid Pigs having trouble making their cash stretch to the end of the month. Fortunately, in 2022, this won't be so much of a problem as you're likely to get a surprise cash boost. This could come in the form of some sort of win, tax rebate, or even an inheritance.

As if that wasn't exciting enough, it even looks as if most Pigs will be back on their travels this year. Anything with a watery theme will be particularly appealing, so think cruises, sea, or lakeside stays or maybe simply renting a villa with its own pool. Whatever you choose, Pig, you're bound to have a ball!

What it Means to Be a Pig

It takes quite a confident person in the West to announce 'I'm a Pig' to an assembled gathering without embarrassment. Imagine the comments! And if they should happen to be at an event where food is being served, they'd never hear the end of the jokes.

Yet, if you were in China and came out with such a remark, chances are you'd get a very favourable response. You'd certainly not be a figure of fun.

The Chinese zodiac Pig – sometimes known as the Boar – is regarded as a lucky sign. Since flesh and blood pigs tend to have very large litters of baby piglets, they're believed to be a symbol of prosperity and plenty.

And given the Chinese fondness for pork, anyone who owned a pig or two would have been fortunate indeed.

What's more, people born in any Year of the Pig tend to be genuinely amiable types – perhaps the most well-liked of all the 12 signs of the zodiac. Cheerful, friendly, and lacking in ego, they have no enemies. They can fit in anywhere. Nobody objects to a Pig.

Pigs just can't help being kind, sympathetic, and tolerant. Should someone let them down, Pigs will just shrug and insist it wasn't their fault. Pigs tend to get let down over and over again by the same people, but it never occurs to them to bear a grudge. They forgive and forget and move happily along. Friends may scold and warn them not to be a soft touch, but Pigs can't help it. They see no point in conflict.

That's not to say it's impossible to annoy a Pig, just that it takes a great deal to rouse the sweet Pig's nature to anger.

The other refreshing thing about the Pig is that they just want to be happy and have a good time – and they usually do. They find fun in the most unpromising situations, and their enthusiasm is infectious. Soon, everyone else is having fun too.

It's true Pigs enjoy their food – perhaps a little too much – but that's because they are a sensuous sign, appreciating physical pleasures; and it makes them very sexy too.

Shopping is a favourite hobby of many Pigs. They're not greedy; they just love spending money on pretty things simply for the sheer delight of discovering a new treasure and taking it home. This sometimes gets the Pig into trouble because finance isn't a strong point, but such is Pig's charm, they usually get away with it.

Pigs don't tend to be madly ambitious. They have no interest in the rat-race yet they are intelligent and conscientious and can't help being highly effective at work, despite having no ulterior motive or game plan. They often end up in managerial roles. Their sympathetic and conciliatory approach, coupled with their willingness to ask others for advice, goes down well in most organisations and usually leads to promotion. What's more, while avoiding unpleasantness wherever possible, the Pig doesn't like to give up on a task once started, and will invariably find a way to get it done that other signs wouldn't have thought of.

The Pig home reflects the sensuous nature of the Pig. Everything will be comfortable and warm with fabrics and furnishings that feel good as well as look good. Items will be chosen for ease of use rather than style, and there will probably be a great many objects and knick-knacks dotted around, picked up on Pig's shopping expeditions. Pigs quite often excel at cooking, and the Pig kitchen is likely to be crammed with all the latest gadgets and devices for food preparation.

Pigs approve of holidays, of course, and take as many as they can. They're not desperate to tackle extreme sports or go on dangerous expeditions, but they can be adventurous too. They like to be out in the open air, especially if it involves picnics and barbecues but, basically, easy-going Pig's just happy to take a break.

Best Jobs for Pig

Patisserie Owner

Party Planner

Cookery Book Compiler

Festival Organiser

Receptionist

PR Consultant

Perfect Partners

Cupid's arrow can strike anywhere at any time, of course, but once the novelty of new romance wears off, some relationships are easier to maintain than others. Here's a guide to the Pig's compatibility with other signs.

Pig with Pig

When one Pig sets eyes on another Pig, they can't help moving closer for a better look, and should they get talking they probably won't stop. These two understand each other and share so many interests and points of view they seem like a perfect couple. Yet, long-term, they can end up feeling too alike. Pigs rarely argue, yet oddly enough they can find themselves squabbling over trivialities with another Pig. Care needed.

Pig with Rat

It's very easy for Rat to be beguiled by the Pig. Pig's easy-going, sympathetic nature immediately relaxes the Rat. What's more, Pig loves shopping as much as Rat so the two of them could enjoy many happy expeditions together. Conflict could occur through overspending. Pig does not understand Rat's compulsion to bag a bargain. Pig will buy whatever the price and the two could end up arguing over money.

Pig with Ox

Delightful Pig will catch Ox's eye, and since Pig isn't a constant thrill-seeker, the two of them could enjoy many peaceful evenings together, perhaps over a tasty meal. Yet Pig's spendthrift ways – at least in Ox's eyes – could soon prove very annoying as well as illogical to the Ox, while Pig could find Ox's attitude judgemental and upsetting. Not ideal for the long-term.

Pig with Tiger

Carefree Pig will love to bask in Tiger's impressive aura, while Tiger will feel good about protecting this charming but unworldly creature. They enjoy each other's company and Tiger, so focused on lofty matters, will find Pig's compulsive shopping too trivial to worry about. This couple could do well together as long as Pig's fondness for cosy nights in doesn't make Tiger feel trapped.

Pig with Rabbit

Pig is not quite as interested in fine dining as Rabbit, and is happy to scoff a burger as much as a cordon bleu creation, but their shared love of the good things in life makes these two happy companions. Once again, Pig's spending habits might irritate Rabbit, but not too much as Rabbit is quite willing to splurge on lovely things for the home. A relationship would work well.

Pig with Dragon

While Dragon and Pig might seem to be opposites, the two of them can create a surprisingly contented relationship. Pig is quite happy for Dragon to fly around doing exciting things as long as Pig is not expected to do much more than admire profusely. Dragon appreciates Pig's uncritical support and makes allowances for Pig's lack of stamina. This couple could live in harmony.

Pig with Snake

Pig and Snake don't have a lot to say to each other. Snake can't be bothered with Pig's endless shopping, and Pig is hurt by Snake's snobbish attitude. They both enjoy the good things in life so a luxury fling could briefly be fun – a shared spa break might be a good idea – but in the long-term, this relationship is probably not worth pursuing.

Pig with Horse

Pig and Horse are good companions. Horse is soothed by easy-going Pig and Pig is proud to be seen with such an alluring creature as Horse. They don't have a lot of interests in common, but they don't antagonise each other either. They can jog along amicably for quite a while, but long-term they may find they each want more than the other can provide.

Pig with Goat

Happy-go-lucky Pig and laid-back Goat make a good pair. They hate to stir up trouble and always look for a peaceful solution to any challenge. Ideally, they'd avoid the challenge altogether. They could be very contented together as long as Pig's spending and Goat's inability to deal with finances doesn't get them into trouble.

Pig with Monkey

On the surface, these two might seem an unlikely couple. Yet Pig enjoys Monkey's fun and humour while Monkey is happy to be admired uncritically. What's more, Monkey's inventive mind can solve any difficulties caused by Pig's spending, and since Monkey can't resist a challenge, the opportunity to retrain Pig or at least find a way to obtain purchases cheaper could help the relationship last.

Pig with Rooster

These two might seem an unlikely couple – modest Pig with extrovert Rooster. Yet Pig has no need or wish to crow, and can see the vulnerable character that lurks beneath Rooster's fine feathers. While Rooster responds to Pig's kindness and undemanding nature. As long as Rooster doesn't get bored, this can be a contented relationship.

Pig with Dog

In the outside world, the dog and the pig can get along well together; in fact, pigs, being intelligent creatures, can do many of the things dogs can do, so it's not surprising this zodiac pair make a good couple. Good-natured Pig is uncomplicated and fair-minded which suits Dog perfectly. Also, Pig brings out Dog's playful side – which delights Pig who's always keen to have a playmate. A happy relationship involving many restaurants.

Pig Love 2022 Style

Sexy, sensuous Pig tends to believe it's love that makes the world go round, and given the chance, will prefer to put more energy into romance than career. Well, this year, you can go right ahead and follow your naughty instincts, Pig. 2022 is made for fun and flirtation as far as your sign is concerned.

Single Pigs will discover brief encounters in an astonishing variety of places. Think supermarket aisles, station platforms, even filling up the car. The chances to come across new partners are not confined to clubs and parties – they are, almost literally, everywhere. For this reason, single Pigs might like to make sure they're looking their best whenever they open their front door (delivery driver anyone?). Yet, in truth, it doesn't matter how you look, Pig. Your natural magnetism draws people to you, whatever you're wearing.

Single Pigs will be having so much fun they're not really thinking of settling down. Yet it's quite possible that somewhere in the stream of new admirers is the one you've been waiting for. Think carefully before you move on.

Attached Pigs, seeing their single cousins enjoying themselves so heartily, could well find themselves getting restless. If your relationship is not what it was, Pig, it might be time to check out the dating scene. If the two of you are basically content, 2022 is the perfect time to inject a little more excitement into the relationship. Use your imagination, Pig!

Secrets of Success in 2022

You don't need to do anything revolutionary to find success this year, Pig. With the good fortune flowing your way from the Tiger, you're all primed and ready to reap countless rewards.

Something you set up, possibly last year, is beginning to grow in a very encouraging way. The signs are good. Just make sure you don't take your eye off the ball! Treating yourself to too many days off, spa sessions, or super-long lunches could cost you dear in more ways than one.

Also, take care to keep business and romance separate. A workplace dalliance may prove tempting and looks very likely this year, but resist at all costs. The repercussions could be messy by 2023.

In a similar vein, there's a strong possibility a lover might try to muscle in on your career in some way. Perhaps they just want to help, or maybe they've got a partnership in mind. Whichever it is, tread warily and don't let them anywhere near your finances. In fact, don't allow them to get involved until you've known them a lot longer.

Finally, as always, vow to keep spending to a minimum, Pig – which in your case is still quite a substantial sum. Cash is coming your way in 2022, but that doesn't mean you have to spend it all the same year!

The Pig Year at a Glance

January – It's a new year, and you're getting good vibes. The outlook is exciting. Check your budget and overhaul if necessary.

February – Treat yourself to a new look. This is the perfect time to revamp your wardrobe, hair, and diet.

March – A fascinating stranger catches your eye. This could be interesting. Work flows smoothly.

April – An unexpected bill arrives. Could this be an error? Investigate carefully before you pay.

May – Jealous eyes are scowling at you. Is this work, romance, or both? Try not to antagonise them. Keep your distance.

June – Someone's trying to interest you in an exercise or health plan. It might be more enjoyable than you think.

July – A friend or partner is planning a trip. Shopping and fine restaurants could be involved. You're in!

August – Holidays beckon. You don't mind where you go, but you need to hit the summer sales.

September – An authority figure signals more effort is needed. They're right – time to buckle down.

October – A friend in need gets in touch. With time, you find the perfect solution to their problem.

November – Many Pigs started Christmas shopping in January, but there's always room for more…

December – Pig festivities are legendary, and this year you excel yourself. The family will be talking about it for months to come.

Lucky colours for 2022: Purple, Silver, Orange

Lucky numbers for 2022: 3, 6, 9

CHAPTER 12: THE RAT

Rat Years

5 February 1924 – 24 January 1925

24 January 1936 – 10 February 1937

10 February 1948 – 28 January 1949

28 January 1960 – 14 February 1961

15 February 1972 – 2 February 1973

2 February 1984 – 19 February 1985

19 February 1996 – 7 February 1997

7 February 2008 – 25 January 2009

25 January 2020 – 11 February 2021

Natural Element: Water

Will 2022 be a Golden Year for the Rat?

Can you feel the temperature rising, Rat? The sparks are beginning to fly for you, and 2022 is the year you could make your name.

Chances are, last year was slow-going if you're typical of your sign, Rat. There were plenty of opportunities, yet you may not have appreciated the tedious pace, and some Rats will have given up on them altogether. Annoyingly, this gradual process was just what you needed after the tumultuous events of 2020 when the Rat was in charge. Most Rats began 2021 feeling drained and badly needed time to wind down.

Well, here you are in 2022, hopefully rested and refreshed and ready for action. And action is what the Tiger has in store!

This year, you are being called upon to stand on your own two feet and take care of everything yourself. In truth, you usually prefer to do things that way, even if it's not necessary. Well, in 2022, it's necessary. It's not that you can't trust other people, or they're not capable (though sometimes they're not); it's just that this year your vision will be the best, and you will be the one person to finish what gets started.

The reason is – although you and the Tiger are not the best of best buddies – you respect each other and have an understanding. Despite the difference in size, you are both very strong personalities, and the Tiger expects a lot from you, Rat. The Tiger tends to be a solitary creature and very self-reliant, and those are the qualities that will be demanded of the Rat, too, this year.

As a result, Rats are set to do exceptionally well at work. This is not the time to change jobs unless it's unavoidable because Rats can now work wonders from within. Big changes are required. Innovative skills, creativity, and a little cunning are called for – all talents the Rat possesses in abundance. This is your chance to step into the limelight, Rat, and show what you can do.

The results will be dazzling. Promotion, pay rises, and a general expansion of your career plans will follow.

The pay rises, in particular, are important because it seems the Rat finances may have lapsed a little lately. This was probably due to overspending, but the good news is you'll be able to restore your savings and add to them in 2022.

It gets even more exciting, Rat, because there's a strong possibility your job will lead to a house move. This may not be permanent, so Rats who adore their present residence need not worry… but it looks as if many Rats will be relocating for career reasons.

You may find you end up as a troubleshooting Rat – dispatched to other areas to restore their fortunes, or you may be transferred for a set period. Whatever the reason, some Rats may buy property in the new location, whilst others could rent, but either way, you'll be spending a lot of time living away from your usual circle.

Another reason you have the 'edge' in a lot of ways at the moment, Rat, is the element of the year, which is Water. As the Rat is regarded as belonging to the Water family of creatures, you are literally *in your element* in 2022! Water is believed to be associated with cash flowing, but also communication and emotions. This year the Water's pouring through in a very powerful form. Some signs might find this a little overwhelming, but not the tough, street-wise Rat. For the Rat, it's invigorating.

As a born communicator, the energy of 2022 allows you to find just the right touch to motivate your colleagues, calm quarrels, and reach out to new clients.

If you're involved in training in any form, or studying for further qualifications, you'll have all the right answers, Rat. No wonder you're the go-to person for almost every issue this year.

In view of the emphasis on career and relocation, Rat, the chances are you've not got much time or inclination for holidays. You'll be doing quite a bit of travelling, but most of it on business. Yet this probably won't faze the typical Rat. A change of scene is almost as good as a break as far as the Rat is concerned, so most Rats will enjoy exploring wherever they happen to find themselves.

It looks like you'll be having a fine time in 2022, Rat; just don't forget to slow down now and then, or the Tiger will wear you out.

What it Means to Be a Rat

It doesn't sound so good does it, to call yourself a Rat? In fact, it may seem strange to start the astrological cycle with such a controversial creature as the unwelcome rodent. Here in the West, we haven't a good word to say about them. We talk of 'plagues' of rats; they 'infest' dirty, derelict places; they hang around dustbins.

They're associated with disease, rubbish, and sewers, and if a rat should be spied near our homes, we'd be straight on the phone to pest control. They make us shudder. Describe a person as 'a rat', and you're certainly not paying them a compliment.

Yet the Chinese view things differently. When they think of the zodiac Rat, they're thinking not of the flea-ridden rodent with the disconcerting long, hairless tail. They're imagining a certain energy, certain admirable qualities they associate with the creature. Rats, after all, are a very successful species. They are great survivors; they're quick, intelligent, tenacious, and they seem to thrive almost anywhere, under any conditions. All excellent qualities to be commended, if you found them in a human.

So, far from being an unfortunate sign, being born in the year of the Rat is regarded as a good omen.

Rats possess great charm and elegance. They're chatty, intelligent, and make friends easily. At parties, people seem drawn to them. There's something about their genuine enjoyment of being surrounded by new faces that makes them easy to get along with. Yet, they value old friends too, will make an effort to stay in touch, and a friendship with a rat is likely to last a lifetime.

Both male and female rats always look good. They believe that outward appearances are important. Instinctively, they understand that you only get one chance to make a first impression, so they take care never to be caught off-guard looking a mess.

This happy knack is easier for them than most because they love shopping and are Olympic-standard bargain hunters. They can't resist a sale and if it's a designer outlet, so much the better. Their homes are usually equally smart for the same reason. Rats have innate good taste and are as thrilled with finding a stylish chair, or piece of artwork at half price, as they are a pair of shoes.

They enjoy spending money and the challenge of hunting down the best deal; and because they're also successful at work, they tend to have plenty of cash to splurge. Yet, despite this, Rats can often be viewed as a bit stingy. They're not mean, it's just that Rats' strong survival instincts lead them to prioritise themselves and their family when it comes to allocating their resources. Within their families, Rats are extremely generous.

Rats also enjoy the finer things in life. They prefer not to get their hands dirty if at all possible and are experts at getting other people to do mundane tasks for them. They like pampering and luxury and lavish holidays. Yet, being supremely adaptable, they will happily embark on a backpacking trip if it takes them where they want to go and there's no other option. They're adventurous, and hate to be bored, so they're prepared to take a calculated risk if some place or person catches their eye.

Yet, this willingness to take a risk combined with the love of a bargain can occasionally get them into trouble, despite their super-sensitive survival instincts. Rats, particularly male Rats, have to guard against the urge to gamble. The combination of the prospect of winning easy money, the excitement of the element of chance, and the challenge of pitting their wits against the odds can prove irresistible. What starts as a mild flirtation for fun can end up as quite a problem.

The same could be said for suspect 'get-rich-quick' schemes. Though clever and sceptical enough to see through them, Rats are so thrilled by the idea of an easy gain, the temptation to cast doubts aside, against their better judgement, can be overwhelming.

But if any sign can get away with such unwise habits, it's probably the Rat. Rats are good at making money and handling money. They're also masters at spotting an escape route and scuttling away down it if the going gets too tough. Underneath that gregarious bonhomie, there's a shrewd, observant brain that misses nothing. Rats have very sharp eyes and are highly observant even when they don't appear to be taking any notice. They are also very ambitious, though they tend to keep it quiet. Dazzled by their genuine charm and witty conversation, people often fail to see that most moves Rats make are taking them methodically to the top. It's no accident they call it 'the rat race'.

Best Jobs for Rats in 2022

Troubleshooter

Estate Agent

Promoter

Events Organiser

Fashion Buyer

Online Trader

Perfect Partners 2022

Cupid's arrow can strike anywhere at any time, of course, but once the novelty of new romance wears off, some relationships are easier to maintain than others. Here's a guide to the Rat's compatibility with other signs.

Rat with Rat

These two are certainly on the same wavelength and share many interests. When their eyes first meet, passionate sparks may fly. This relationship could work very well, though over time the competitive and ambitious nature of both partners could see them pulling in different directions. What's more, if one should succumb to a weakness for gambling or risky business ventures while the other does not, it will end in tears.

Rat with Ox

Oddly enough, this combination can be surprisingly successful. Frenetic Rat and calm Ox may seem to be opposites but, in fact, Rat can find Ox's laid-back approach strangely soothing. Ox is not interested in competing with Rat and will put up with Rat's scurrying after new schemes with patience. As long as Rat doesn't get bored and has enough excitement in other areas of life, this relationship could be very contented.

Rat with Tiger

The magnificent Tiger will always catch Rat's eye because Rat loves beautiful things, but Tiger's natural element is Wood and Rat's is Water which means that Tiger wears Rat out. What's more, Tiger's not interested in Rat's latest bargain, and Rat doesn't share Tiger's passion for changing the world, yet the attraction is strong. If Rat makes an effort to step back and not get in Tiger's way, they could reach a good understanding.

Rat with Rabbit

Rat finds Rabbit intriguing. Here is an attractive, stylish creature that doesn't feel the need to be pushy or take centre stage yet somehow manages to be at the heart of things. The Rat wants to find out more, while Rabbit is flattered and entertained by witty Rat's attention. These two respect each other but, over the long-term, Rat could be too overpowering.

Rat with Dragon

This couple is usually regarded as a very good match. They have much in common being action-loving, excitement-seeking personalities who hate to be bored. It takes a lot to dazzle Rat, but the Dragon's glamorous aura proves irresistible, while Dragon loves to be admired, so each enjoys being with the other. There could be the odd power struggle as these two are both strong characters, but the magnetism is so powerful they usually kiss and make up.

Rat with Snake

The Snake shares Rat's good taste and being elegant, sophisticated, and smart will delight Rat at first sight. These two get on very well on an intellectual level but perhaps are better as good friends rather than long-term partners. The Snake's love of basking in the sun for hours strikes Rat as lazy and dull, while Rat's need to rush around doing deals and meeting people seems pointless and wearying to the Snake.

Rat with Horse

Rat and Horse both fizz with energy and they love action and looking good, yet this is not seen as an ideal partnership. Nothing's impossible, of course, but these two will have to work hard to find harmony. The Rat will admire Horse's enthusiasm and cheerful approach but become impatient to discover Horse can also be fiery and emotional. Horse, on the other hand, can find Rat's risk-taking behaviour extremely worrying.

Rat with Goat

The Rat is charmed by carefree Goat and fascinated by its artistic talent and happy knack of living in the present. Easy-going Goat tends to like everyone so is perfectly content to enjoy Rat's company. These two can get along fine, yet they don't really understand each other deep down. Long-term, the Rat may find Goat's lack of interest in the practical side of life, such as finances and bills, irritating.

Rat with Monkey

Unlikely as it might appear, mischievous Monkey and the clever Rat make a good partnership. Their quick minds, sociable natures, and love of novelty ensure that they're never bored together. True, Rat might sometimes feel Monkey is too inclined to skim over the surface of things and could do with being more serious at times, but Monkey's ingenuity and audaciousness always save the day. Both can have a weakness for gambling though, so need to take care.

Rat with Rooster

The first thing Rat notices about the Rooster is its beautiful plumage, but this a relationship which is unlikely to get much further than initial admiration. Rooster's direct and frank approach can strike the Rat as tactless, while the Rooster can't understand why Rat has to make life so convoluted and complicated. Then again, Rooster's natural confidence and aplomb can come across as bragging to the Rat. These two have to be very determined to make a partnership work.

Rat with Dog

The Rat and the Dog get along pretty well together. Both are strong characters, and they respect each other and give each other space when required. But deep down, the Dog is a worrier and gets anxious about unnecessary risks, while Rat just can't help sailing close to the wind if an interesting opportunity presents itself. Long-term, reckless Rat might unintentionally drive Dog to distraction. Only to be considered by Dogs with nerves of steel.

Rat with Pig

It's very easy for Rat to be beguiled by the Pig. Pig's easy-going, sympathetic nature immediately relaxes the Rat. What's more, Pig loves shopping as much as Rat so the two of them could enjoy many happy expeditions together. Conflict could occur through overspending. Pig does not understand Rat's compulsion to bag a bargain. Pig will buy at whatever the price and the two could Love

Rat Love 2022 Style

Whenever there's a gathering, you can be sure the Rat will be there – the centre of attention – handing out the drinks and making everyone laugh. Naturally, the single Rat catches everyone's eye, and they can have their pick of partners.

Yet, surprisingly, the single Rat doesn't always take advantage of romance. Their mind is more likely to be mulling over some career conundrum than noticing a new admirer.

Last year, many single Rats were concentrating on building their careers and – this year – their careers are more likely to be building them! A different emphasis but same result as far as the Rat's love life is concerned.

Since you're likely to be moving around a lot this year, Rat, new relationships will be more difficult to maintain. On the other hand, you'll get the chance to meet a whole fresh circle – possibly several – so someone very special could come into your life this year; someone whose path would never normally have crossed yours.

Attached Rats may have to quell a little discontent on the home-front this year. By now, your partner has probably got used to the way you're so involved in your career – if they haven't, they're probably no longer your partner – but now you're talking about either moving or working away. This could be awkward, Rat. If it's true love, however, you'll find a way!

Secrets of Success in 2022

It's not much of a secret for you this year, Rat… your route to the top is becoming crystal clear. Even if you're not given the official title of 'boss', you're put in charge of very important career matters in 2022. The future of the business could depend on you – seriously.

Yet, there's no cause for alarm because you know how to make this work. You need to be decisive, conscientious, and responsible, yet diplomatic and understanding with clients and colleagues. You've also got to take a few risks as far as new technology and novel approaches go.

Still, these are simple matters for the typical Rat – particularly the taking risks part. Unlike some other signs, you're not afraid of a small gamble where career is concerned.

It's not impossible for you to mess things up, Rat, but if you do, any failure is likely to be due to the way you spend your downtime. After so much hard work and responsibility, it's only natural the Rat needs to de-stress, but too many late nights, too much partying, an over-indulgence in online gambling – all tempting treats for the typical Rat – could lead to disaster.

If you think 'restraint' in your leisure time, Rat, and resist the urge to cut corners to save time at work – nothing can stop you this year.

The Rat Year at a Glance

January – Lots of sleepy heads around you, Rat, yet you're raring to go. Work off some energy in a boot camp.

February – What happened? You're flavour of the month at work. A new project has put in your charge.

March – Friends and colleagues need an energising influence. You can supply it, and then some.

April – Your career is thriving; your talents are needed more widely. Relocation could be on the cards.

May – Friction with friends and family seems unavoidable. Could it be work-related? Time to talk.

June – You could be exploring new places. Work or pleasure? Consider your options carefully.

July – A new face at work appeals. No harm in getting to know them, but keep it professional.

August – Everyone's talking holidays, but you're too busy. It might be an idea to take a break, though, Rat… even just a day or two.

September – Cash is rolling in, but expenses are piling up. Streamline your outgoings, Rat.

October – A timid person in your orbit is trying to hold you back. They'll see sense; be patient.

November – The boss is smiling, and things are on the up. Take a bow, Rat. You've turned the tide.

December – Christmas? What Christmas? No, you don't need to be a Grinch this year, Rat. Great celebrations all around.

Lucky colours for 2022: Blue, Red and Silver

Lucky numbers for 2022: 2, 6

CHAPTER 13: THE OX

Ox Years

25 January 1925 – 12 February 1926

11 February 1937 – 30 January 1938

29 January 1949 – 16 February 1950

15 February 1961 – 4 February 1962

3 February 1973 – 22 January 1974

20 February 1985 – 8 February 1986

8 February 1997 – 27 January 1998

26 January 2009 – 13 February 2010

12 February 2021 – 31 January 2022

Natural Element: Water

Will 2022 be a Golden year for the Ox?

Okay, Ox, you can officially climb down from the stage, hand back your 'I'm in charge – the buck stops here!' badge, and go off to enjoy a well-earned break.

To be honest, although (in many ways) you enjoyed running the show, you're probably relieved to be handing over the responsibility to another sign. It's been a long 12 months, and though you're renowned for your amazing stamina, you deserve a rest.

If you're typical of your sign, you've probably done pretty well – in a non-flashy sort of way – during 2021. The Ox has never been devoted to travel and tends to feel holidays are over-rated, so the restrictions and lockdowns of the previous year won't have bothered you. In fact, many an Ox has discovered a new appreciation for their home and neighbourhood surroundings while relishing the chance to get a ton of work done.

The good news about 2022, for the Ox, is that you're about to start reaping the rewards of all that effort. The flowing Water of this year's sign is going to wash a great deal of cash your way – as long as you put in the hard work in 2021… which, of course, the typical Ox did!

Your career is likely to blossom now and colleagues will, for once, finally recognise how valuable your contribution has been. It's recognition that's often overlooked because you don't make a big deal of your achievements and tend to leave the limelight to more pushy types. This year, the Tiger's sense of justice and fair play will change all that for you.

Promotion and pay rises are likely to be yours, and if you decide to take your skills to another company, you'll be welcomed with open arms.

So, what's not to like, you might be thinking? Well, the not quite so good news is that, despite these benefits, you and the boss of the year – the Tiger – are not exactly best mates.

The Tiger doesn't dislike you; it's just that you are opposites when it comes to temperament and the way you like to do things. For a start, the Tiger prefers to dash about, leaping from one project to the next – one person to the next, quite often, as well.

This is horrifying to the typical Ox. The Ox likes to do one thing at a time, properly and thoroughly, while remaining loyal to their circle. Yet, in 2022, the pressure is on to make changes, to expand and explore new horizons.

Many an Ox will find this atmosphere stressful or even worrying. The speed of these changes could be particularly unsettling, too.

The reason for this, from the astrological point of view, lies in the fact that every sign is believed to belong to its own natural 'element'. The Ox is regarded as a Water creature, while the Tiger is reckoned to be a Wood animal. Since Water is believed to feed and nourish Wood to help it grow, Water creatures like the Ox can find Wood animal years literally draining, though they can't quite put their finger on why.

There's something about Tiger energy that can wear Ox out. So even though your strength is legendary, Ox, it would be a good idea to pace yourself in 2022.

We're talking about a Black Water Tiger here, of course, and the Water element of the year, in harmony with Ox sensibilities, will help diminish the effect of helping all that Wood. Basically, this Tiger year will be better for Ox than most.

Yet, Water is also associated with emotions and communication so, with a double helping (as it were), expect to be unusually emotional this year, Ox. Ideally, this will manifest in a boost for loving, romantic relationships but be careful because it could also lead some Ox to take offence where none is intended and stomp off in extended sulks.

You'll also find friends you didn't realise you had appearing out of nowhere, wanting to spend time with you. Even better, many of them will be eager to help with whatever project you've got in mind. In spite of yourself, you're set to find you're caught up in an unaccustomed social whirl.

You're still not desperate to go on holiday, of course, but may find yourself dragged away by friends or family all the same. And this year you'll actually enjoy it!

Most of all, quite a few Ox will escape the pressures by relocating to new homes in quieter areas. With all that extra cash coming your way, Ox, you can probably afford an upgrade to Ox Towers. Rural views – or at least the sight of flowers and trees outside the window – are particularly beneficial for Ox; so, when choosing a new place, think Green.

Finally, as you shelter in a tranquil haven watching Tiger hurtle by, you might find this is the ideal time to add to the family. A baby calf in the home would be the perfect end to 2022.

What it Means to Be an Ox

Okay, so hands up everyone who's secretly disappointed to be an astrological Ox?

Sounds a bit bovine and boring, doesn't it? The Ox might lack the glamour of the Tiger or the Dragon. It can't even boast the intriguing notoriety of a sign like the Rat or the Snake. In fact, here in the West, we may not even be entirely sure what an Ox looks like. Some sort of large cow, perhaps?

So, at first sight, you might be excused for thinking the Ox was dull. Yet, in China, that wasn't the perception at all. There was a very good reason the Ox was so highly placed – at number two – on the zodiac wheel.

The animal was revered as essential to country life. So precious, it was regarded as a gift from the Gods. So special, in fact, it's said that in the past the Chinese didn't eat beef. They couldn't possibly disrespect such an important beast by serving it up for dinner.

So, while the Ox may not seem as exciting as some of the other celestial animals, the sign of the Ox is respected and appreciated.

What the Chinese valued was the phenomenal strength and endurance of the Ox. Get an Ox moving, and it will plod on mile after mile, covering huge distances with apparent ease and without complaint. Without the work of the Ox, many a family would have gone hungry.

People born in the year of the zodiac Ox are believed to be blessed with similar qualities. For this reason, though unflashy and quietly spoken, they often end up being extremely successful in whatever they undertake – from their career to their favourite hobby, or creating a harmonious family that blossoms.

Oxen have a wonderful knack of planning a sensible, logical course to wherever they want to go and then following it, relentlessly, step by step until they get there, no matter what obstacles they encounter en-route. Oxen find it rather puzzling that other people can't seem to adopt the same simple approach. They don't understand why some signs give up before reaching their goal. Why do they waste their time chopping and changing and getting nowhere, wonders the Ox.

Ox patience is legendary. They may not be quick, or nimble, but they realise that slow, steady, consistent effort achieves far more in the long run. And the Ox is only interested in the long haul. At heart, the Ox is serious-minded, and though they enjoy a joke as much as anyone else, they regard frivolity as a pleasant diversion, not an end in itself.

Ox people are usually good-looking in a healthy, wholesome way, but they're not impressed by flashy, passing whims and fashions. Superficial gloss has no appeal. The Ox woman is unlikely to be found rocking extreme, designer clothes or wafting fingers iridescent with the latest nail polish.

Ox tastes tend to be classic and practical. They are instinctively private and hate to draw attention to themselves, yet the Ox is one of the nicest signs. Genuinely honest, kind, and sincere, Ox is ready to help anyone in trouble, happily pitching in to lend a hand without expecting anything in return. Yet, since Ox tends to speak only when they have something to say, other signs can find them difficult to get to know. It's worthwhile making the effort because the Ox will be a loyal friend forever.

What's more, when they do have something to say, Ox views can be surprisingly frank. Just because they are patient and kind, it doesn't mean they can be pushed around. The Ox is self-reliant and makes up its own mind; it's not swayed by the opinions of others. What's more, they can be very stubborn. When the Ox finally makes a decision, it sees no reason to change it.

Ox people are not materialistic. They work hard because the task interests them, or because they can see it needs to be done, and they will keep going until the project is complete. They are the true craftsmen of the zodiac, excelling in working with their hands and they can be unexpectedly artistic and innovative when the occasion demands. As a result, money can accumulate and Ox is not averse to spending it on some creature comforts. The Ox home will be warm and styled for comfort and practicality rather than cutting-edge design. If there's no space for a garden, it's likely to be filled with houseplants too, because Ox has green fingers and needs to see nature close at hand.

Travel and holidays are not top of the Ox agenda; they enjoy their work and their home and are not forever itching to get away. Unlike many signs, they cope with routine very well. And for all their modesty and quiet diligence, there is always something impressive about the Ox. Other signs sense the latent strength and power that lies just below the surface and tend not to impose too much. This is just as well because though the Ox may appear calm, placid, and slow to anger, when they do finally lose their temper, it can be terrifying. What's more, the Ox will never forget an insult and can bear a grudge for years. Ox doesn't stay mad – they get even.

Best Jobs for Ox 2022

Potter

Animal Trainer

Garden Designer

Nurse

Financial Adviser

Auctioneer

Jewellery Maker

Plumber

Dressmaker

Web Designer

Perfect Partners

Cupid's arrow can strike anywhere at any time, of course, but once the novelty of new romance wears off, some relationships are easier to maintain than others. Here's a guide to the Ox's compatibility with other signs.

Ox with Ox

These two could be very happy together, as long as one of them plucks up the courage to admit they're interested. Sloppy, sentimental romance is not their style and they both share this view so there'll be no misunderstandings around Valentine's Day. They know that still waters run deep and they can enjoy great contentment without showy declarations of love.

Ox with Tiger

Not an easy match. Ox and Tiger could be on different planets. Fiery Tiger doesn't frighten Ox and Tiger may admire Ox's strong, good looks and sincere nature but they both need different things from life. Tiger wants to dash about changing the world for the better, while Ox reckons you get more done by buckling down where you happen to be and attending to the details. Clashes could abound.

Ox with Rabbit

Ox finds Rabbit rather cute and appealing. Whether male or female there's something about Rabbit's inner fluffiness that brings out Ox's highly developed protective instincts. Rabbit meanwhile loves the Ox's reassuring presence and the sense of security Ox provides. These two could get on very well together as long as refined Rabbit can overlook Ox's occasional down-to-earth – Rabbit might say 'coarse' - observations.

Ox with Dragon

Chalk and cheese though this pair may appear to be there's a certain fascination between them. Ox may not approve of Dragon's showy manner but recognises Dragon's good intentions, while Dragon admires Ox's strength of character and gift for completing tasks. If each could find a way to tolerate the other's wildly different lifestyles, they might be good for each other, but long term, Dragon's hectic pace might wear even the Ox's legendary stamina.

Ox with Snake

Like Ox, the Snake is quietly ambitious and not given to racing around unless it's absolutely necessary. Ox, on the other hand, respects Snake's clever brain and understated elegance. These two could quickly discover how beneficial an alliance between them would be. They're both happy to give the other space when required but also step in with support when needed. This could be a very successful match.

Ox with Horse

Long ago, on many Western farms, Ox was replaced by the Horse and it may be that Ox has never forgotten and never forgiven. At any rate, these two, despite both being big, strong animals, are not usually friends. Horse is too flighty and frivolous to interest Ox for long, while Ox's methodical, careful ways will irritate the Horse. Best not to go there.

Ox with Goat

Though these two share artistic natures even if in the case of the Ox, they're well hidden, deep down, they don't 'get' one another. Ox may be beguiled at first by Goat's friendly, easy-going manner but then disappointed to discover Goat seems to find everyone equally delightful, even those who're plainly unworthy. Goat, on the other hand, can't understand why Ox won't lighten up more. This relationship would require a lot of effort and compromise.

Ox with Monkey

The naughty Monkey scandalises Ox, but in such an amusing way that Ox can't help laughing. Monkey, on the other hand, is equally amused to find an audience so easy to shock. This unlikely pair enjoy each other's company and get on surprisingly well. Yet, right from the start, it's probably obvious to both that a long term relationship couldn't last. A fun flirtation, though, could be a terrific tonic for them both.

Ox with Rooster

For all its bravado and showing off, the Rooster is a down-to-earth type, drawn to security and accumulating the good things in life – requirements that Ox understands very well and can supply effortlessly. What's more, Ox can't help but admire Rooster's fine feathers and skill at communicating in a crowd – attributes Ox doesn't have and is unlikely to acquire. These two could enjoy a very good partnership.

Ox with Dog

These two ought to get along well as they're both sensible, down to earth, loyal and hardworking and in tune with each other's basic beliefs. And yet, somehow, they don't. Dog has a playful streak and finds this lacking in Ox, while Ox may be baffled by what seems like pointless silliness in Dog. If they can agree to differ, they could make a relationship work.

Ox with Pig

Delightful Pig will catch Ox's eye, and since Pig isn't a constant thrill-seeker, the two of them could enjoy many peaceful evenings together, perhaps over a tasty meal. Yet Pig's spendthrift ways – at least in Ox's eyes, could soon prove very annoying as well as illogical to the Ox, while Pig could find Ox's attitude judgemental and upsetting. Not ideal for the long term.

Ox with Rat

Oddly enough, this combination can be surprisingly successful. Frenetic Rat and calm Ox may seem to be opposites, but in fact Rat can find Ox's laid-back approach strangely soothing. Ox is not interested in competing with Rat and will patiently put up with Rat's scurrying after new schemes. As long as Rat doesn't get bored and generates enough excitement in other areas of life, this relationship could be very contented.

Ox Love 2022 Style

There's no avoiding it, Ox, this year you're going to be in demand, but for different reasons to your popularity last year. You were the King or Queen of 2021 back then, so of course your premier position attracted a lot of fans and also hangers-on. As a modest Ox, you might even have found the attention a bit overwhelming.

After all, the typical Ox prefers quality to quantity when it comes to partners. Ox prefers to gaze longingly from afar at some super-fit apparition, discreetly learning as much as possible about the beloved before making a move. Well, that tactic might still prove a bit difficult 12 months on. You're no longer the ruler of the year, but as we're awash with the Water element in 2022 and you are a Water sign, your enigmatic charms are still powerfully appealing.

The enhanced emotion swirling around you at the moment will have sympathetic types desperate to cheer you up or protect you from harm.

Single Oxen will have their pick of partners, and Oxen already in relationships can lay back and allow their loved one to pamper them. They will still have to watch out for jealousy in these emotional months – either theirs or their partner's – but handled with care, the turbulence can be avoided.

The good news is that solid, happy partnerships are set to flourish, and new additions to the family are a distinct possibility. Single Oxen might even take a tip from the Tiger and enjoy playing the field for a while.

Secrets of Success in 2022

You may no longer be boss of the year, Ox, but that doesn't mean you can't do brilliantly in 2022. Quite the opposite. Your talents are in great demand right now, plus you're set to be showered with golden rewards that you earned last year but which were held up in the general chaos. What's more, new opportunities are opening up all around you – you only need to open your eyes, see them for what they are, and go for them!

In fact, the only thing that can hold you back is your own attitude. Let's face it, you're not the most flexible of signs. In many ways, this is one of your strengths… if you say you'll do something, people can absolutely depend on you to keep your word – a rare and admirable quality. Yet if you're a typical Ox, this means it often takes you a while to get used to changes. After all, when you've got things the way you want them, why mess them around unnecessarily? The 'if it ain't broke, don't fix it' approach makes perfect sense to you.

This year, however, the Tiger demands a rethink – at speed. It might not be 'broke', but chances are it could be improved. If you can overcome that stubborn streak and agree to take a fresh look at your routine or your business, examine it from a different perspective, and imagine all the ways you could tweak the detail, you might be amazed at the results. Some creative new thinking could produce something really spectacular with Tiger energy behind you, so don't scoff – give it a try!

Finally, with so much emotional Water slopping around, you might find yourself getting all soppy and sentimental one minute and seething with outrage the next. You're not going crazy. Just take a deep breath, relax, and concentrate on being the winner you're destined to become.

The Ox Year At a Glance

January – The last month at the helm, and you're a little frazzled. Ease up and enjoy the rest of the limelight.

February – Everyone around might be partying, but there's no rush. Bide your time and check out the changes developing around you.

March – A colleague is getting extra friendly. Do you need their help? Not necessarily, but it's good to have another ally.

April – A bust-up in the workplace threatens. The boss is getting difficult. Time to dust off your diplomatic skills.

May – Romance is getting interesting, but a rival could be trying to muscle in. Don't stoop to their level.

June – A friend turns to you in turmoil. You don't think of yourself as an agony aunt, but your input could work wonders.

July – An arty type arrives on the scene, and you're not sure how things will pan out. Combine your talents, and you could be quite a team.

August – Even the boss reckons you should take some holiday. Why not give it a go?

September – An irritating newcomer annoys you. Try not to get worked up. Keep your head down and ignore them.

October – Busy, busy, busy. You've got a ton to do, and romance is blossoming too. Not enough hours in the day.

November – Oops. You've taken your eye off the ball, and finances need sorting. Yet those luxuries look tempting…

December – Christmas is coming, and you're pleased with your progress. You can afford to treat the family to some fun festivities.

Lucky colours for 2022: Blue, Orange, Silver

Lucky numbers for 2022: 2, 5

CHAPTER 14: BUT THEN THERE'S SO MUCH MORE TO YOU

So now you know your animal sign, but possibly you're thinking – okay, but how can everyone born in the same year as me have the same personality as me?

You've only got to think back to your class at school, full of children the same age as you, to know this can't be true. And you're absolutely right. What's more, Chinese astrologers agree with you. For this reason, in Chinese astrology, your birth year is only the beginning. The month you were born and the hour of your birth are also ruled by the twelve zodiac animals – and not necessarily the same animal that rules your birth year.

These other animals then go on to modify the qualities of your basic year personality. So someone born in an extrovert Tiger year but at the time of day ruled by the quieter Ox, and in the month of the softly spoken Snake, for instance, would very likely find their risk-taking Tiger qualities much toned down and enhanced by a few other calmer, more subtle traits.

By combining these three important influences, you get a much more accurate and detailed picture of the complex and unique person you really are. These calculations lead to so many permutations it soon becomes clear how people born in the same year can share various similarities, yet still remain quite different from each other.

What's more, the other animals linked to your date of birth can also have a bearing on how successful you will be in any year and how well you get on with people from other signs. Traditionally, the Horse and the Rabbit don't get on well together, for instance, so you'd expect two people born in these years to be unlikely to end up good friends. Yet if both individuals had other compatible signs in their charts, they could find themselves surprisingly warming to each other.

This is how it works:

Your Outer Animal – (Birth Year | Creates Your First Impression)

You're probably completely unaware of it, but when people meet you for the first time, they will sense the qualities represented by the animal that ruled your birth year. Your Outer Animal and its personality influence the way you appear to the outside world. Your Outer animal is your public face. You may not feel the least bit like this creature deep down, and you may wonder why nobody seems to understand the real you. Why is it that people always seem to underestimate you, or perhaps overestimate you, you may ask yourself frequently. The reason is that you just can't help giving the impression of your birth-year animal and people will tend to see you and think of you in this way – especially if they themselves were born in other years.

Your Inner Animal – (Birth Month I The Private You)

Your Inner Animal is the animal that rules the month in which you were born. The personality of this creature tells you a lot about how you feel inside, what motivates you, and how you tend to live your life. When you're out in the world and want to present yourself in the best light, it's easy for you to project the finest talents of your birth-year animal. You've got them at your fingertips. But at home, with no one you need to impress, your Inner Animal comes to the fore. You can kick back and relax. You may find you have abilities and interests that no one at work would ever guess. Only your closest friends and loved ones are likely to get to know your Inner Animal.

By now you know your Outer Animal so you can move on to find your Inner Animal from the chart below:

Month of Birth - Your Inner Animal

January – the Ox

February – the Tiger

March – the Rabbit

April – the Dragon

May – the Snake

June – the Horse

July – the Goat

August – the Monkey

September – the Rooster

October – the Dog

November – the Pig

December – the Rat

Your Secret Animal – (Birth Hour | The Still, Small Voice Within)

Your secret animal rules the time you were born. Each 24-hour period is divided into 12, two-hour time-slots and each slot is believed to be ruled by a particular animal. This animal represents the deepest, most secret part of you. It's possibly the most intimate, individual part of you as it marks the moment you first entered the world and became 'you'. This animal is possibly your conscience and your inspiration. It might represent qualities you'd like to have or sometimes fail to live up to. Chances are, no one else will ever meet your Secret Animal.

For your Secret Animal check out the time of your birth:

Hours of Birth – Your Secret Animal

1 am – 3 am – the Ox

3 am – 5 am – the Tiger

5 am – 7 am – the Rabbit

7 am – 9 am – the Dragon

9 am – 11 am – the Snake

11 am – 1.00 pm – the Horse

1.00 pm – 3.00 pm – the Goat

3.00 pm – 5.00 pm – the Monkey

5.00 pm – 7.00 pm – the Rooster

7.00 pm – 9.00 pm – the Dog

9.00 pm – 11.00 pm – the Pig

11.00 pm – 1.00 am – the Rat

When you've found your other animals, go back to the previous chapters and read the sections on those particular signs. You may well discover talents and traits that you recognise immediately as belonging to you in addition to those mentioned in your birth year. It could also be that your Inner Animal or your Secret Animal is the same as your Year animal. A Dragon born at 8 am in the morning, for instance, will be a secret Dragon inside as well as outside, because the hours between 7 am and 9 am are ruled by the Dragon.

When this happens, it suggests that the positive and the less positive attributes of the Dragon will be held in harmony, so this particular Dragon ends up being very well balanced.

You might also like to look at your new animal's compatibility with other signs and see where you might be able to widen your circle of friends and improve your love life.

CHAPTER 15: IN YOUR ELEMENT

There's no doubt about it, Chinese astrology has many layers. But then we all recognise that we have many facets to our personalities, too. We are all more complicated than we might first appear. And more unique, as well.

It turns out that even people who share the same Birth Year sign are not identical to people with the same sign but born in different years. A Rabbit born in 1963, for instance, will express their Rabbit personality in a slightly different way to a Rabbit born in 1975. This is not simply down to the influence of the other animals in their chart, it's because each year is also believed to be ruled by one of the five Chinese 'elements', as well as the year animal.

These elements are known as Water, Wood, Fire, Earth, and Metal.

Each element is thought to contain special qualities which are bestowed onto people born in the year it ruled, in addition to the qualities of their animal sign.

Since there are 12 signs endlessly rotating, and five elements, the same animal and element pairing only recurs once every 60 years. Which is why babies born in this 2022 Year of the Black Tiger are unlikely to grow up remembering much about other Black Tigers from the previous generation. Those senior Tigers will already be 60-years-old when the new cubs are born.

In years gone by, when life expectancy was much lower, the chances are there would only ever be one generation of a particular combined sign and element alive in the world at a time.

Find Your Element from the Chart Below:

The 1920s

5 February 1924 – 24 January 1925 | RAT | WOOD

25 January 1925 – 12 February 1926 | OX | WOOD

13 February 1926 – 1 February 1927 | TIGER | FIRE

2 February 1927 – 22 January 1928 | RABBIT | FIRE

23 January 1928 – 9 February 1929 | DRAGON | EARTH

10 February 1929 – 29 January 1930 | SNAKE | EARTH

The 1930s

30 January 1930 – 16 February 1931 | HORSE | METAL

17 February 1931 – 5 February 1932 | GOAT | METAL

6 February 1932 – 25 January 1933 | MONKEY | WATER

26 January 1933 – 13 February 1934 | ROOSTER | WATER

14 February 1934 – 3 February 1935 | DOG | WOOD

4 February 1935 – 23 January 1936 | PIG | WOOD

24 January 1936 – 10 February 1937 | RAT | FIRE

11 February 1937 – 30 January 1938 | OX | FIRE

31 January 1938 – 18 February 1939 | TIGER | EARTH

19 February 1939 – 7 February 1940 | RABBIT | EARTH

The 1940s

8 February 1940 – 26 January 1941 | DRAGON | METAL

27 January 1941 – 14 February 1942 | SNAKE | METAL

15 February 1942 – 4 February 1943 | HORSE | WATER

5 February 1943 – 24 January 1944 | GOAT | WATER

25 January 1944 – 12 February 1945 | MONKEY | WOOD

13 February 1945 – 1 February 1946 | ROOSTER | WOOD

2 February 1946 – 21 January 1947 | DOG | FIRE

22 January 1947 – 9 February 1948 | PIG | FIRE

10 February 1948 – 28 January 1949 | RAT | EARTH

29 January 1949 – 16 February 1950 | OX | EARTH

The 1950s

17 February 1950 – 5 February 1951 | TIGER | METAL

6 February 1951 – 26 January 1952 | RABBIT | METAL

27 January 1952 – 13 February 1953 | DRAGON | WATER

14 February 1953 – 2 February 1954 | SNAKE | WATER

3 February 1954 – 23 January 1955 | HORSE | WOOD

24 January 1955 – 11 February 1956 | GOAT | WOOD

12 February 1956 – 30 January 1957 | MONKEY | FIRE

31 January 1957 – 17 February 1958 | ROOSTER | FIRE

18 February 1958 – 7 February 1959 | DOG | EARTH

8 February 1959 – 27 January 1960 | PIG | EARTH

The 1960s

28 January 1960 – 14 February 1961 | RAT | METAL

15 February 1961 – 4 February 1962 | OX | METAL

5 February 1962 – 24 January 1963 | TIGER | WATER

25 January 1963 – 12 February 1964 | RABBIT | WATER

13 February 1964 – 1 February 1965 | DRAGON | WOOD

2 February 1965 – 20 January 1966 | SNAKE | WOOD

21 January 1966 – 8 February 1967 | HORSE | FIRE

9 February 1967 – 29 January 1968 | GOAT | FIRE

30 January 1968 – 16 February 1969 | MONKEY | EARTH

17 February 1969 – 5 February 1970 | ROOSTER | EARTH

The 1970s

6 February 1970 – 26 January 1971 | DOG | METAL

27 January 1971 – 14 February 1972 | PIG | METAL

15 February 1972 – 2 February 1973 | RAT | WATER

3 February 1973 – 22 January 1974 | OX | WATER

23 January 1974 – 10 February 1975 | TIGER | WOOD

11 February 1975 – 30 January 1976 | RABBIT | WOOD

31 January 1976 – 17 February 1977 | DRAGON | FIRE

18 February 1977 – 6 February 1978 | SNAKE | FIRE

7 February 1978 – 27 January 1979 | HORSE | EARTH

28 January 1979 – 15 February 1980 | GOAT | EARTH

The 1980s

16 February 1980 – 4 February 1981 | MONKEY | METAL

5 February 1981 – 24 January 1982 | ROOSTER | METAL

25 January 1982 – 12 February 1983 | DOG | WATER

13 February 1983 – 1 February 1984 | PIG | WATER

2 February 1984 – 19 February 1985 | RAT | WOOD

20 February 1985 – 8 February 1986 | OX | WOOD

9 February 1986 – 28 January 1987 | TIGER | FIRE

29 January 1987 – 16 February 1988 | RABBIT | FIRE

17 February 1988 – 5 February 1989 | DRAGON | EARTH

6 February 1989 – 26 January 1990 | SNAKE | EARTH

The 1990s

27 January 1990 – 14 February 1991 | HORSE | METAL

15 February 1991 – 3 February 1992 | GOAT | METAL

4 February 1992 – 22 January 1993 | MONKEY | WATER

23 January 1993 – 9 February 1994 | ROOSTER | WATER

10 February 1994 – 30 January 1995 | DOG | WOOD

31 January 1995 – 18 February 1996 | PIG | WOOD

19 February 1996 – 7 February 1997 | RAT | FIRE

8 February 1997 – 27 January 1998 | OX | FIRE

28 January 1998 – 5 February 1999 | TIGER | EARTH

6 February 1999 – 4 February 2000 | RABBIT | EARTH

The 2000s

5 February 2000 – 23 January 2001 | DRAGON | METAL

24 January 2001 – 11 February 2002 | SNAKE | METAL

12 February 2002 – 31 January 2003 | HORSE | WATER

1 February 2003 – 21 January 2004 | GOAT | WATER

22 January 2004 – 8 February 2005 | MONKEY | WOOD

9 February 2005 – 28 January 2006 | ROOSTER | WOOD

29 January 2006 – 17 February 2007 | DOG | FIRE

18 February 2007 – 6 February 2008 | PIG | FIRE

7 February 2008 – 25 January 2009 | RAT | EARTH

26 January 2009 – 13 February 2010 | OX | EARTH

The 2010s

14 February 2010 – 2 February 2011 | TIGER | METAL

3 February 2011 – 22 January 2012 | RABBIT | METAL

23 January 2012 – 9 February 2013 | DRAGON | WATER

10 February 2013 – 30 January 2014 | SNAKE | WATER

31 January 2014 – 18 February 2015 | HORSE | WOOD

19 February 2015 – 7 February 2016 | GOAT | WOOD

8 February 2016 – 27 January 2017 | MONKEY | FIRE

28 January 2017 – 15 February 2018 | ROOSTER | FIRE

16 February 2018 – 4 February 2019 | DOG | EARTH

5 February 2019 – 24 January 2020 | PIG | EARTH

The 2020s

25 January 2020 – 11 February 2021 | RAT | METAL

12 February 2021 – 1 February 2022 | OX | METAL

2 February 2022 – 21 January 2023 | TIGER | WATER

22 January 2023 – 9 February 2024 | RABBIT | WATER

10 February 2024 – 28 January 2025 | DRAGON | WOOD

29 January 2025 – 16 February 2026 | SNAKE | WOOD

17 February 2026 – 5 February 2027 | HORSE | FIRE

6 February 2027 – 25 January 2028 | GOAT | FIRE

26 January 2028 – 12 February 2029 | MONKEY | EARTH

13 February 2029 – 2 February 2030 | ROOSTER | EARTH

You may have noticed that the 'natural' basic element of your sign is not necessarily the same as the element of the year you were born. Don't worry about this. The element of your birth year takes precedence, though you could also read the qualities assigned to the natural element as well, as these will be relevant to your personality but to a lesser degree.

Metal

Metal is the element associated in China with gold and wealth. So if you are a Metal child, you will be very good at accumulating money. The Metal individual is ambitious, even if their animal sign is not particularly career-minded. The Metal-born version of an unworldly sign will still somehow have an eye for a bargain or a good investment; they'll manage to buy at the right time when prices are low and be moved to sell just as the price is peaking. If they want to get rid of unwanted items, they'll potter along to a car boot sale and without appearing to try, somehow make a killing, selling the lot while stalls around them struggle for attention. Career-minded signs with the element Metal have to be careful they don't overdo things. They have a tendency to become workaholics. Wealth will certainly flow, but it could be at the expense of family harmony and social life.

The element of Metal adds power, drive, and tenacity to whatever sign it influences so if you were born in a Metal year you'll never lack cash for long.

Water

Water is the element associated with communication, creativity, and the emotions. Water has a knack of flowing around obstacles, finding routes that are not obvious to the naked eye and seeping into the smallest cracks. So if you're a Water child, you'll be very good at getting what you want in an oblique, unchallenging way. You are one of nature's lateral thinkers. You are also wonderful with people. You're sympathetic, empathetic, and can always find the right words at the right time. You can also be highly persuasive, but in such a subtle way nobody notices your influence or input. They think the whole thing was their own idea.

People born in Water years are very creative and extremely intuitive. They don't know where their inspiration comes from, but somehow ideas just pour into their brains. Many artists were born in Water years.

Animal signs that are normally regarded as a little impatient and tactless have their rough edges smoothed when they appear in a Water year. People born in these years will be more diplomatic, artistic, and amiable than other versions of their fellow signs. And if you were born in a naturally sensitive, emotional sign, in a Water year, you'll be so intuitive you're probably psychic. Yet just as water can fall as gentle nurturing rain, or a raging destructive flood, so Water types need to take care not to let their emotions run away with them or to allow themselves to use their persuasive skills to be too manipulative.

Wood

Wood is the element associated with growth and expansion. In Chinese astrology, Wood doesn't primarily refer to the inert variety used to make floorboards and furniture, it represents living, flourishing trees and smaller plants, all pushing out of the earth and growing towards the sky.

Wood is represented by the colour green, not brown. If you're a Wood child, you're likely to be honest, generous, and friendly. You think BIG and like to be involved in numerous projects, often at the same time.

Wood people are practical yet imaginative and able to enlist the support of others simply by the sincerity and enthusiasm with which they tackle their plans. Yet even though they're always busy with a project, they somehow radiate calm, stability, and confidence. There's a sense of the timeless serenity of a big old tree about Wood people. Other signs instinctively trust them and look to them for guidance.

Animal signs that could be prone to nervousness or impulsive behaviour tend to be calmer and more productive in Wood year versions, while signs whose natural element is also Wood could well end up leaders of vast teams or business empires. Wood people tend to sail smoothly through life, but they must guard against becoming either stubborn or unyielding as they grow older or alternatively, saying 'yes' to every new plan and overextending themselves.

Fire

Fire is the element associated with dynamism, strength, and persistence. Fire demands action, movement, and expansion. It also creates a huge amount of heat. Fire is precious when it warms our homes and cooks our food, and it possesses a savage beauty that's endlessly fascinating. Yet it's also highly dangerous and destructive if it gets out of control. Something of this ambivalent quality is evident in Fire children.

People born in Fire years tend to be immensely attractive, magnetic types. Other signs are drawn to them. Yet there is always a hint of danger, of unpredictability, about them. You never know quite where you are with a Fire year sign and in a way, this is part of their fascination.

People born in Fire years like to get things done. They are extroverted and bold and impatient for action. They are brilliant at getting things started and energising people and projects. Quieter signs born in a Fire year are more dynamic, outspoken, and energetic than their fellow sign cousins, while extrovert signs positively blaze with exuberance and confidence when Fire is added to the mix.

People born in Fire years will always be noticed, but they should try to remember they tend to be impatient and impulsive. Develop a habit of pausing to take a deep breath to consider things, before rushing in, and you won't get burned.

Earth

Earth is the element associated with patience, stability, and practicality. This may not sound exciting but, in Chinese astrology, Earth is at the centre of everything: the heart of the planet. Earth year children are strong, hardworking personalities. They will persist with a task if it's worthwhile and never give up until it's complete. They create structure and balance, and they have very nurturing instincts.

Women born in Earth years make wonderful mothers, and if they're not mothering actual children, they'll be mothering their colleagues at work, or their friends and relatives, while also filling their homes with houseplants and raising vegetables in the garden if at all possible.

Other signs like being around Earth types as they exude a sense of security. Earth people don't like change, and they strive to keep their lives settled and harmonious. They are deeply kind and caring and immensely honest. Tact is not one of their strong points, however. They will always say what they think, so if you don't want the unvarnished truth, better not to ask!

Earth lends patience and stability to the more flighty, over-emotional signs, and rock solid integrity to the others. Earth people will be sought-after in whatever field they choose to enter, but they must take care not to become too stubborn. Make a point of seeking out and listening to a wide range of varying opinions before setting a decision in stone.

Yin and Yang

As you looked down the table of years and elements, you may have noticed that the elements came in pairs. Each element was repeated the following year. If the Monkey was Water one year, it would be followed immediately the next year by the Rooster, also Water.

This is because of Yin and Yang – the mysterious but vital forces that, in Chinese philosophy, are believed to control the planet and probably the whole universe. They can be thought of as positive and negative, light and dark, masculine and feminine, night and day, etc. but the important point is that everything is either Yin or Yang; the two forces complement each other and both are equally important because only together do they make up the whole. For peace and harmony to be achieved, both forces need to be in balance.

Each of the animal signs is believed to be either Yin or Yang and because of the need for balance and harmony, they alternate through the years. Six of the 12 signs are Yin and six are Yang and since Yang represents extrovert, dominant energy, the Yang sign is first, followed by the Yin sign which represents quiet, passive force. A Yang sign is always followed by a Yin sign throughout the cycle.

The Yang signs are:

Rat

Tiger

Dragon

Horse

Monkey

Dog

The Yin Signs are

Ox

Rabbit

Snake

Goat

Rooster

Pig

Although Yang is seen as a masculine energy, and Yin a feminine energy, in reality, whether you are male or female, everyone has a mixture of Yin and Yang within them. If you need to know, quickly, whether your sign is Yin or Yang just check your birth year. If it ends in an even number (or 0) your sign is Yang. If it ends in an odd number, your sign is Yin.

In general, Yang signs tend to be extrovert, action-oriented types while Yin signs are gentler, more thoughtful, and patient.

So, as balance is essential when an element controls a period of time, it needs to express itself in its stronger Yang form in a Yang year as well as in its gentler Yin form in a Yin year, to be complete.

This year of the Black Water Tiger opens a new round of the Water element in its Yang form, which then completes next year in its Yin form with the Water Rabbit.

But why do elements have two forms? It's to take into account the great variations in strength encompassed by an element. The difference between a candle flame and a raging inferno – both belonging to Fire; or a great oak tree and a little seedling – both belonging to the Wood element.

In Yang years, the influence of the ruling element will be particularly strong. In Yin years, the same element expresses itself in its gentler form.

Friendly Elements

Just as some signs get on well together and others don't, so some elements work well together while others don't. These are the elements that exist in harmony:

METAL likes EARTH and WATER

WATER likes METAL and WOOD

WOOD likes WATER and FIRE

FIRE likes WOOD and EARTH

EARTH likes FIRE and METAL

The reason for these friendly partnerships is believed to be the natural, productive cycle. Water nourishes Wood and makes plants grow, Wood provides fuel for Fire, Fire produces ash which is a type of Earth, Earth can be melted or mined to produce Metal while Metal contains or carries Water in a bucket.

So, Water supports Wood, Wood supports Fire, Fire supports Earth, Earth supports Metal and Metal supports Water.

Unfriendly Elements

But since everything has to be in balance, all the friendly elements are opposed by the same number of unfriendly elements. These are the elements that are not in harmony:

METAL dislikes WOOD and FIRE

WATER dislikes FIRE and EARTH

WOOD dislikes EARTH and METAL

FIRE dislikes METAL and WATER

EARTH dislikes WOOD and WATER

The reason some elements don't get on is down to the destructive cycle which is: Water puts out Fire and is absorbed by Earth, Wood breaks up Earth (with its strong roots) and is harmed by Metal tools, Metal is melted by Fire and can cut down Wood.

So if someone just seems to rub you up the wrong way, for no logical reason, it could be that your elements clash.

CHAPTER 16: WESTERN HOROSCOPES AND CHINESE HOROSCOPES – THE LINK

So now, hopefully, you'll have all the tools you need to create your very own, personal, multi-faceted Chinese horoscope. But does that mean the Western-style astrological sign that you're more familiar with is no longer relevant?

Not necessarily. Purists may not agree, but the odd thing is there does seem to be an overlap between a person's Western birth sign and their Chinese birth month sign; the two together can add yet another interesting layer to the basic birth year personality.

A Rabbit born under the Western sign of Leo may turn out to be very different on the surface, to a Rabbit born under the Western sign of Pisces for instance.

Of course, Chinese astrology already takes this into account by including the season of birth in a full chart, but we can possibly refine the system even further by adding the characteristics we've learned from our Western Sun Signs into the jigsaw.

If you'd like to put this theory to the test, simply find your Chinese year sign and then look up your Western Astrological sign within it, from the list below. While you're at it, why not check out the readings for your partner and friends too? You could be amazed at how accurate the results turn out to be.

Ox

Aries Ox

Dynamic Aries brings the Ox a very welcome blast of fire and urgency to stir those methodical bones into faster action. This is a fortunate combination because when the steadfast, industrious, patient qualities of the Ox are combined with quickness of mind and a definite purpose, very little can stand in the way of this subject's progress. Aries Oxen do particularly well in careers where enormous discipline combined with flair and intelligence is required. Many writers are born under this sign as are college lecturers, historical researchers and archaeologists.

Taurus Ox

Oxen are notoriously stubborn creatures but combine them with Taurus the bull and this trait is doubled if not quadrupled. It is not a good idea to box these types into a corner because they will take a stand and refuse to budge even if the house is on fire. Taurean Oxen really will cut off their noses to spite their faces if they feel they have to. Fall out with them and stop talking, and the chances are that the feud will continue to the grave. Yet despite this tendency, Oxen born under the sign of Taurus are not unfriendly types. They are utterly reliable and totally loyal. Family and friends trust them completely. They might be a bit old fashioned and inflexible, but they are lovable too.

Gemini Ox

Chatty Gemini transforms the normally taciturn Ox into a beast which is almost loquacious, at least by the normal standards of these strong silent types. They might even be confident enough to attempt a few jokes, and though humour is not the Oxen's strongpoint, the Gemini Ox can usually produce something respectably amusing if not sidesplittingly funny. Oddly enough, should the Ox set his mind to it and apply his awesome hard work and patience to the subject of humour he might even make a career of it. Some Gemini Oxen have even become accomplished comedians – not simply through natural talent but through sheer hard work and perseverance. More frequently, however, the combination of Gemini with the Ox produces a 'poor man's lawyer' – a highly opinionated individual who can see what's wrong with the government and the legal system and loves to put the world to rights at every opportunity.

Cancer Ox

Oxen born under the sign of Cancer can go very far indeed, not through the application of brainpower although they are by no means unintelligent, but through the skills they have at their fingertips. These subjects are the craftsmen of the universe. Diligent, painstaking, and precise, they are incapable of bodging any practical task they undertake. They will spend hours and hours honing whatever craft has taken their fancy until they reach what looks to others like the peak of perfection. The Cancer Ox won't accept this of course. He can detect the minutest flaw in his own handiwork, but when he is finally forced to hand it over, everyone else is delighted with his efforts. Many artists, potters and sculptors are born under this sign.

Leo Ox

When the Lion of Leo meets the enormous strength of the Ox, the result is a formidable individual, indeed. Annoy or mock these powerful types at your peril. And anyone who dares to pick a fight with the Lion-Ox is likely to come out of it very badly. Most of the time, however, Leo is a friendly lion bringing confidence and a more relaxed attitude to the unbending Ox. These types are more broad-minded and open-hearted than the usual Oxen. They have been known to enjoy parties and once tempted into the limelight they may even find it's not as bad as they feared. In fact, secretly, they're having a ball.

Virgo Ox

Oxen born under the sign of Virgo tend to be very caring types. Though they show their feelings in practical ways and shun sloppy, emotional displays you can rely on an Ox born under Virgo to comfort the sick, help the old folk and notice if anyone in the neighbourhood needs assistance. Florence Nightingale could have been a Virgo Ox. The unsentimental but immensely useful and humane work she did for her sick soldiers is typical of these types. They make excellent nurses and careworkers, forever plumping pillows, smoothing sheets and knowing just the right touches to bring comfort where it is needed. On a personal level, these subjects are inclined to be critical and easily irritated by the small failings of others, but their bark is worse than their bite. Their kindness shines through.

Libra Ox

Generally speaking the down to earth Ox has little time for putting on the charm. As far as Ox is concerned, people either like you or they don't, and it's not worth worrying about it either way. There's no point in wasting valuable time trying to bend your personality to accommodate the whims of others. Yet when the Ox is born under the sign of Libra, this trait is modified somewhat. Libra people just can't help having charm even if they are Oxen and therefore express that charm more brusquely than usual. The Libran Ox glides effortlessly through life, pleasing others without even realising it. These types are sympathetic and like to help those in need wherever possible. Try to take advantage of their good nature or trick them with an untrue sob story, though, and they will never forgive you.

Scorpio Ox

The typical Ox is notoriously difficult to get to know, and when that Ox happens to be born under the secretive sign of Scorpio, you might as well give up and go home. You'll learn nothing from this creature unless he has some special reason for telling you. Stubborn and silent, these types are very deep indeed; they care nothing for the opinions of others and follow their own impenetrable hearts come what may. However, win the love of one of these unique subjects, and you have a very rare prize indeed. You will unlock a devotion and passion that you have probably never experienced before and will probably never experience again. This is a strangely compelling combination.

Sagittarius Ox

The Ox born under Sagittarius is a more carefree type than his brothers and sisters. Something of the free spirit of the horse touches these subjects, and while there is no chance of them kicking up their heels or doing anything remotely irresponsible, they at least understand these temptations in others and take a more relaxed view of life. The Ox born under Sagittarius is ambitious but independent. These types don't like to be told what to do and are probably more suited to being self-employed than working for others. They are more easy-going than a lot of Oxen and for this reason attract a wider range of friends. Like their Gemini cousins, they might even hazard a joke from time to time. All in all, the Ox born under Sagittarius gets more fun out of life.

Capricorn Ox

Unlike his Sagittarian brother, the Ox born under Capricorn takes himself and life very seriously indeed. These types usually do very well in material terms and often end up in positions of authority; yet if they're not careful, they can look burned out. With good reason. Capricorn Oxen have never learned how to relax, and they see life as a struggle; consequently, for them, it is. Yet they have much to be glad for. They are great savers for a rainy day, and so they never have to worry about unpaid bills, their capacity for hard work is so enormous they can hardly help but achieve a great deal, and before very long they find themselves well off and regarded with respect by everyone in the community. If these types could only manage to unwind, be gentle with themselves and enjoy their success, they could be very happy indeed.

Aquarius Ox

The Ox has never been a flashy sign. These types believe actions speak louder than words, and they like to beaver away without drawing attention to themselves. When this trait is coupled with the slightly introverted though idealistic nature of Aquarius, you get a quiet, complex character who prefers to work behind the scenes and turns modest when the limelight is switched on. Never known for his verbal dexterity, the Ox born under Aquarius can suddenly turn into a persuasive orator when a humanitarian cause sparks unexpected passion. These types make loyal, faithful companions to those who take the trouble to understand them and their intelligence and dogged persistence makes them invaluable as researchers, political assistants and private secretaries.

Pisces Ox

Few Oxen can be described as fey, changeable creatures but those that come the closest will be found under the sign of Pisces. Pisces brings an emotional, artistic quality to the steadfast Ox. These types are loving, faithful and true, yet it is often difficult to guess what they are thinking. Of all the Ox family, Pisces Oxen are likely to be the most moody and yet in many ways also the most creative. The Ox input lends strength and stamina to more delicate Pisces constitutions, enabling them to accomplish far more than other Pisces subjects. Just leave them alone until they're ready to face the world.

Tiger

Aries Tiger

Another combination which could be potentially explosive but in this case, energetic Aries adds force and power to the Tiger's humanitarian instincts while the Tiger's unworldly nature curbs Aries materialistic streak. These types really could change the world for the better if they put their minds to it. They are kind and thoughtful, and while they might be impatient at times, they quickly regret any harsh words spoken in the heat of the moment.

Taurus Tiger

Taurus Tigers are tremendous achievers. The strength of the zodiac bull added to the fire of the Tiger produces a truly formidable individual who can do almost anything to which he sets his mind. These types often end up making a great deal of money. They have to work hard for all their gains, but this doesn't worry them at all. They also take a great deal of pleasure in spending their hard-earned cash. They like to share what they've got, and this gives them such childish joy that no-one begrudges them their good fortune.

Gemini Tiger

The quicksilver mind of Gemini adds zing and extra flexibility to the Tiger's powerful individualism. These Tigers are blessed with minds which overflow with brilliant ideas. They are creative and often artistic too, so they're capable of wonderful achievements. Their only drawback is that they possess almost too much of a good thing. They have so many ideas that they tend to zoom off at a tangent onto a new task before they have completed the one on which they were working.

Cancer Tiger

These Tigers are immensely clever but a little more retiring than the usual bold, brave terror of the jungle. No Tiger is timid, but Cancer has the effect of quietening the more reckless excesses of the Tiger and allowing a little caution to creep into the blend. They still like a challenge but will opt for something a little less physically demanding than other Tigers. These types are more able to fit into society and tolerate authority better than other Tigers, and for this reason they often do well in their careers.

Leo Tiger

What would you get if you crossed a lion with a tiger? A very wild beast indeed. Some sort of striped wonder of the world no doubt! Leo Tigers certainly make their mark. Tigers are big, beautiful, fearless personalities who crave the limelight and love to be noticed. They believe in doing good deeds, but they like to be noticed doing them. These are not the types of which anonymous benefactors are made. When the Leo Tiger raises money for charity, he likes to make sure the world's press are gathered to record the occasion if at all possible. Yet his heart's in the right place. Let these Tigers have their share of praise, and they will work wonders for others.

Virgo Tiger

The Virgo Tiger is quite a different beast. Virgo accentuates the Tiger's already well-developed sense of justice. These types cannot rest until wrongdoers have got their just deserts. They often go into professions involving the law and the police force. They are immensely self-disciplined and have very high standards. Totally trustworthy and effective, they can sometimes be a little difficult to live with. They are not unkind; it's just that they expect everyone else to be as perfect as they are themselves. Yet Virgo adds attention-to-detail to Tiger's passion to change the world, and the combination creates a character who really could make a lasting difference.

Libra Tiger

Laidback Libra brings quite a different quality to the Tiger. Tiger's intensity is softened by pure Libra charm, and the result is a Tiger of unrivalled compassion and magnetism. Libra Tigers often end up in the caring professions where people flock to them with relief. These Tigers want to help, and Libra gives them the ability to understand just what people need and when. You'd never catch a Libra Tiger helping an old lady across the road who didn't wish to go. Libra Tiger would realise at once that the woman was waiting for a bus, would stand with her to keep her company, help her on when the vehicle arrived and make sure the driver put her off at the right stop. No wonder these Tigers are so well-loved wherever they go.

Scorpio Tiger

Crossing a Scorpion with a Tiger is a very tricky proposition. These types mean well, but they are often misunderstood. Scorpio brings a tremendous depth of feeling to the Tiger's reforming instincts, but this sometimes causes them to put tremendous effort into the wrong causes with alarming results. These types can be very quick-tempered, and they may nurse a grudge for a long time. They never forgive disloyalty, and they never forget. It would be a serious mistake to make an enemy of a Scorpio Tiger – but once this individual becomes a friend, they'll be loyal for life.

Sagittarius Tiger

Another charmer, the Sagittarius Tiger is nevertheless likely to hit the road at the slightest opportunity. These types are wanderers, and no matter how much they seem to enjoy company, they enjoy moving on even more. They can't bear working for other people and do far better being self-employed. The travel industry would suit them perfectly. Impossible to cage in or pin down – don't even try – the only way to have a happy relationship with a Sagittarius Tiger is to make them feel free at all times.

Capricorn Tiger

Steady Capricorn lends a prudent touch to the impulsive Tiger, and these types are the Tigers most likely to stop and think before rushing off to save the rain forest. They still enjoy improving the world, but they check travel arrangements, make sure they have got sufficient funds and do a bit of research online first. These are not party animals. While they enjoy company, they prefer serious discussion to frivolous small talk and much as they enjoy travel they appreciate the comfort of home. These Tigers like to develop their theories from the depths of their favourite armchair beside their own cosy hearth.

Aquarius Tiger

When idealistic Aquarius meets idealistic Tiger, you have to hang onto that long tiger tail to keep these subjects, feet on the ground. These types really do have their heads in the clouds and are totally unpredictable. Once a worthwhile cause presents itself, they will rush off immediately without a thought to the consequences. Convention is of no interest to them. They couldn't care less what other people think. They go through life guided entirely by a strong inner sense of right and wrong. If it's right, they know it without a shadow of a doubt; if it's wrong, they will not do it no matter what anyone says. This attitude can get them into a lot of trouble, but other signs sneakily admire their courage. People may not agree with Aquarius Tiger, but no one can doubt his integrity.

Pisces Tiger

One of Tiger's failings is a tendency to be indecisive without warning, and this trait is heightened in Pisces Tigers. These types are anxious to do the right thing; it's just that sometimes it's very difficult to know what that right thing is. There are so many alternatives. Pisces Tiger is kind and gentle and apt to get sentimental at times. They want to save the world, but they'd like someone alongside to help them – though not too many. Despite their indecision, they usually end up heading in the right direction in the end. Yet, even when they've achieved a great deal, they still agonise over whether they could have done even more.

Rabbit

Aries Rabbit

This is a very dynamic Rabbit. When powerful Aries injects a streak of energy into that cultured Rabbit personality, the result is a wonderfully clever individual who glides effortlessly to success. Although at times Aries Rabbit has an attack of over-cautiousness, these types are usually bolder than the average bunny and achieve much where other Rabbits might run away. Occasionally, these Rabbits will even take a gamble, and this is worthwhile as it usually pays off for them.

Taurus Rabbit

The Taurus Rabbit really does feel his home is his castle. He is not unduly interested in his career, but he is likely to turn his home into an art form. Brilliant entertainers, these types guarantee their lucky guests will enjoy all the creature comforts possible. They often marry later in life than average, but when they do, they work at the relationship. Providing they choose another home bird, they are likely to be very happy.

Gemini Rabbit

All Rabbits are natural diplomats, but the Gemini Rabbit really is the star of them all. So skilled a communicator is this creature, so expert at people management that a career in the diplomatic service, politics, psychology or even advertising is an option. Never lost for words, these types can persuade anyone to do almost anything. As a result, they are usually very successful. Once they harness their enviable skills to a worthwhile career, they can go far.

Cancer Rabbit

Cancer Rabbits are gentle, kindly souls. They like to be surrounded by pleasant company and prefer to have few demands put upon them. They don't really take to business life and find many professions too abrasive. On the other hand, they find working for themselves too stressful a venture to be considered seriously. They are happiest in a peaceful, routine environment where they can make steady progress, but really their hearts are at home. Home is where they express themselves.

Leo Rabbit

Leo Rabbits, on the other hand, are usually very popular with a wide circle of friends. Extrovert Leo gives Rabbit a strong dose of confidence and flair, and when these qualities are added to Rabbit's people skills, a radiant, magnetic individual is born. Leo Rabbits adore parties where they shine. They are always elegant and beautifully turned out and have a knack of putting others at their ease. These Rabbits climb the ladder of success very quickly.

Virgo Rabbit

Virgo Rabbits have a lot on their minds. The natural cautiousness of the Rabbit is heightened by the same quality in Virgo, and these Rabbits tend to be born worriers. They are masters of detail but, unfortunately, this often leads them to make mountains out of molehills. They are very talented creatures but too often fail to make the best use of their gifts because they spend so much time worrying about all the things that could go wrong. If they can learn to relax and take the odd risk now and then, they will go far.

Libra Rabbit

Art-loving Libra blends easily into the cultured sign of the Rabbit. These types love to learn more about beautiful things, and they like to share their knowledge with others. They are so good with people that they can convey information effortlessly and make the dullest subject sound interesting. These types are often gifted teachers and lecturers though they would find difficult inner-city schools too traumatic. Give these types willing and interested pupils, and they blossom.

Scorpio Rabbit

Rabbits tend to be discreet people, and Scorpio Rabbits are the most tight-lipped of the lot. Scorpio Rabbits have a lot of secrets, and they enjoy keeping them. It gives them a wonderful feeling of superiority to think that they know things others don't. They have many secret ambitions too, and they don't like to speak of them in case others are pessimistic and pour scorn on their plans. So it is the Scorpio Rabbit who is most likely to surprise everyone by suddenly reaching an amazing goal that no-one even knew he was aiming for.

Sagittarius Rabbit

Sporty Sagittarius brings a whole new dimension to the art-loving Rabbit. Rabbits are often indoor creatures, but Sagittarian Rabbits are much more adventurous in the open air than the usual bunny. They are sensuous and fun and attract many friends. They are also versatile and can turn their hands to several different careers if necessary. They like to get out and about more than most Rabbits and they are usually very successful.

Capricorn Rabbit

Capricorn Rabbits are great family folk. They firmly believe the family is the bedrock of life, and they work hard to keep their relations happy and together. The Capricorn Rabbit home is the centre of numerous clan gatherings throughout the year and weddings, birthdays, anniversaries and christenings are very important to them. Capricorn Rabbit will never forget the dates. These types are particularly interested in the past and will enjoy researching a family tree going back generations. If it ever crosses their minds that the rest of the tribe seems to leave all the donkey work to Capricorn Rabbit, he'd never say so. And, in truth, he doesn't really mind. There's nothing he loves more than having his family around him.

Aquarius Rabbit

The Aquarius Rabbit is a contradictory creature being both cautious and curious at the same time. These types crave security and love, and yet they have a great longing to find out more about everything around them. Fascinated by art, science and new inventions they love to potter about in book shops and tinker in the shed at home. Once they get an idea in their head, they can't rest until they have experimented with it, frequently forgetting to eat while they work. They need love and understanding.

Pisces Rabbit

The Pisces Rabbit is another bunny who needs a lot of understanding. Often gifted artistically they can sometimes be stubborn and awkward for no apparent reason. Yet when they are in the right frame of mind, they can charm the birds off the trees. It takes them a long time to make a friend, but when they do, it is a friend for life. The Pisces Rabbit home is full of beautiful things, and these subjects love to invite their most trusted friends to come and enjoy the magic.

Dragon

Aries Dragon

The Dragon is already a powerful sign, but when the lively influence of Aries is added, you have a positively devastating individual. These are the types that others either love or loathe. Strong, confident people can cope happily with the Aries Dragon, but more timid souls are terrified. The Aries Dragon himself is quite unaware of the reaction he causes. He goes busily on his way oblivious of the earthquakes all around him. These types have to guard against arrogance, particularly since they have quite a lot to be arrogant about. They also have a tendency to get bored easily and move on to new projects without completing the old, which is a pity since they can accomplish much if they persevere.

Taurus Dragon

There is something magnificent about the Taurus Dragon. Large, expansive types, they move easily around the social scene spreading bonhomie wherever they go. Not the most sensitive of individuals, they find it difficult to assess the moods of others and assume everyone else feels the same way they do. Should it be brought to their attention that someone is unhappy, however, they will move heaven and earth to cheer them up. These types are reliable and conscientious and always keep their promises.

Gemini Dragon

Dragons may not have the quickest minds in the Chinese zodiac, but Gemini Dragons are speedier than most. They are jovial types with a brilliant sense of humour. In fact, they can cleverly joke others into doing what they want. These types have no need for physical force to get their own way; they use laughter instead. At times, Gemini Dragons can be almost devious, which is unusual for a Dragon but nobody really minds their schemes. They give everyone such a good time on the way it's worth doing what they want for the sheer entertainment.

Cancer Dragon

Cautious Cancer and flamboyant Dragon make a surprisingly good combination. Cancer holds Dragon back where he might go too far, while Dragon endows the Crab with exuberance and style. These types like to help others make the most of themselves, but they are also high achievers in their own right. Without upsetting anyone, Cancer Dragons tend to zoom to the top faster than most.

Leo Dragon

This Dragon is so dazzling you need sunglasses to look at him. The proud, glorious Lion combined with the magnificent Dragon is an extraordinary combination, and it's fortunate it only comes around once every twelve years. Too many of such splendid creatures would be hard to take. Leo Dragons really do have star quality, and they know it. They demand to be the centre of attention and praise is like oxygen to them – they can't live without it. Yet they have generous hearts, and if anyone is in trouble, Leo Dragon will be the first to rush to their assistance.

Virgo Dragon

Unusually for a Dragon, the Virgo variety can get quite aggressive if crossed, but this doesn't often happen as very few people would dare take on such a daunting beast. These types are immensely clever in business. They steadily add acquisition to shrewd acquisition until they end up seriously rich. They are wilier than most Dragons who have a surprisingly naive streak, and they make the most of it. These types just can't help becoming successful in whatever they undertake.

Libra Dragon

Dragons are not usually too bothered about trifles such as fine clothes and wallpaper. In fact, some older, more absent-minded Dragons have been known to go shopping in their slippers having forgotten to take them off. The exception is the Dragon born under the sign of Libra. These types are more down to earth and see the sense in putting on a good show for others. They take the trouble to choose smart clothes and keep them looking that way at all times. They are also more intuitive and are not easily fooled by others.

Scorpio Dragon

Handling money is not a Dragon strong point, but the Scorpio variety has more ability in this direction than most. Scorpio Dragons enjoy amassing cash. Rather like their legendary namesakes who hoard treasure in their lairs, Scorpio Dragons like to build substantial nest-eggs and keep them close at hand where they can admire them regularly. These types can also be a little stingy financially, not out of true meanness but simply because they don't like to see their carefully guarded heap diminish in size. Once they understand the importance of a purchase, however, they can be just as generous as their brothers and sisters.

Sagittarius Dragon

When Sagittarius joins the Dragon, the combination produces a real livewire, a true daredevil. The antics of the Sagittarius Dragon, when young, will give their mothers nightmares and later drive their partners to drink. These types can't resist a challenge, particularly a dangerous one. They will climb mountain peaks, leap off cliffs on a hang-glider and try a spot of bungee-jumping to enliven a dull moment. It's no good expecting these types to sit down with a good book; they just can't keep still. However, surrounded by friends, dashing from one perilous venture to the next, the Sagittarius Dragon is one of the happiest people around.

Capricorn Dragon

The Capricorn Dragon looks back at his Sagittarian brother in horror. He simply can't understand the need for such pranks. Being Dragons, these types are bold, but the influence of Capricorn ensures that they are never foolhardy. They look before they leap and occasionally miss a good deal because they stop to check the fine print. They are not the most intuitive of creatures, but show them a needy soul and they will efficiently do whatever's necessary to help. The Capricorn Dragon is a highly effective creature.

Aquarius Dragon

Happy go lucky types, the Aquarius Dragons are usually surrounded by people. Honest and hardworking, they will put in just as much effort for very little cash as they will for a great deal. If someone asks them to do a job and they agree to do it, they will move heaven and earth to fulfil their obligations even if it is not in their best interests to do so. However, they're not suited to routine, and if a task doesn't interest them, they will avoid it at all costs no matter how well paid it might be. Not particularly interested in money for its own sake, these types are sociable and easy to get along with. They are often highly talented in some way.

Pisces Dragon

Pisces Dragons, on the other hand, are surprisingly good with cash. Despite their often vague, good-humoured exteriors these types have excellent financial brains and seem to know just what to do to increase their savings. They are first in the queue when bargains are to be found, and they seem to sense what the next money-making trend is going to be before anyone else has thought of it. These types often end up quite wealthy and excel, particularly, in artistic fields.

Snake

Aries Snake

Generally speaking, Snakes tend to lack energy, so the influence of dynamic Aries is very welcome indeed. These subjects are highly intelligent, well-motivated and never leave anything unfinished. They are achievers and will not give up until they reach their goal – which they invariably do. Nothing can stand in the way of Aries Snakes, and they reach the top of whatever tree they climb.

Taurus Snake

In contrast, the sensuous Taurus Snake really can't be bothered with all that hard work. Taurus Snakes have great ability, but they will only do as much as is necessary to acquire the lifestyle they desire, and then they like to sit back and enjoy it. Tremendous sun worshippers, the Taurus Snakes would be quite happy to be on a permanent holiday, providing the accommodation was a five-star hotel with a fabulous restaurant.

Gemini Snake

The Gemini Snake can be a slippery customer. A brilliant brain, linked to a shrewd but amusing tongue, these types can run rings around almost everybody. They can scheme and manipulate if it suits them and pull off all sorts of audacious tricks but having achieved much, they tend to get bored and lose interest, giving up on the brink of great things. This often leads to conflict with business associates who cannot understand such contradictory behaviour. Insane they call it. Suicidal. The Gemini Snake just shrugs and moves on.

Cancer Snake

The Snake born under the sign of Cancer is a more conventional creature. These types will at least do all that is required of them and bring their formidable Snake brains to bear on the task in hand. They are gifted researchers, historians and archaeologists – any career which involves deep concentration and patient study. But the Cancer Snake must take care to mix with cheerful people since left to himself he has a tendency for melancholy. Warmth, laughter, and plenty of rest transforms the Cancer Snake and allows those unique talents to blossom.

Leo Snake

The Leo Snake is a very seductive creature. Beautifully dressed, sparklingly magnetic, few people can take their eyes off these types, and they know it. All Snakes are sensuous, but the Snake born under the sign of Leo is probably the most sensuous of the lot. Never short of admirers, these types are not eager to settle down. Why should they when they're having such a good time? Late in life, the Leo Snake may consent to get married if their partner can offer them a good enough life. If not, these types are quite content to go it alone – probably because they are never truly on their own. They collect willing followers right into old age.

Virgo Snake

The Virgo Snake is another fascinating combination. Highly intuitive and wildly passionate, the Virgo Snake is all elegant understatement on the outside and erotic abandon on the inside. The opposite sex is mesmerised by this intriguing contradiction and just can't stay away. Virgo Snakes can achieve success in their careers if they put their minds to it, but often they are having too much fun flirting and flitting from one lover to the next. Faithfulness is not their strong point, but they are so sexy they get away with murder.

Libra Snake

When you see a top model slinking sinuously down the catwalk, she could very well be a Libra Snake. Snakes born under this sign are the most elegant and stylish of the lot. They may not be conventionally good looking, but they will turn heads wherever they go. These types really understand clothes and could make a plastic bin-liner look glamorous just by putting it on. Somehow they have the knack of stepping off a transatlantic flight without a crease and driving an open-topped sports car without ruffling their hair. No-one knows quite how they achieve these feats, and Libra Snake isn't telling.

Scorpio Snake

The Snake born under Scorpio is destined to have a complicated life. These types enjoy plots and intrigues, particularly of a romantic nature and spend endless hours devising schemes and planning subterfuge. That ingenious Snake brain is capable of brewing up the most elaborate scams, and there's nothing Scorpio Snake loves more than watching all the parts fall into place. But schemes have a knack of going wrong, and schemers have to change their plans and change them again to cope with each new contingency as it arises. If he's not careful, the Scorpio Snake can become hopelessly embroiled in his own plot.

Sagittarius Snake

Traditionally other signs are wary of the Snake and tend to hold back a little from them without knowing why. When the Snake is born under Sagittarius, however, the subject seems more approachable than most. Sagittarian Snakes sooner or later become recognised for their wisdom and down to earth good sense and people flock to them for advice. Without ever intending to, the Sagittarius Snake could end up as something of a guru attracting eager acolytes desperate to learn more.

Capricorn Snake

The Snake born under Capricorn is more ambitious than the average serpent. These types will reach for the stars and grasp them. Obstacles just melt away when faced with the dual-beam of Capricorn Snake intelligence and quiet persistence. These Snakes are good providers and more dependable than most Snakes. They often end up surrounded by all the trappings of success, but they accomplish this so quietly, no one can quite work out how they managed it.

Aquarius Snake

Another highly intuitive Snake. Independent but people-loving Aquarius endows the serpent with greater social skills than usual. These types attract many friends, and they have the ability to understand just how others are feeling without them having to say a word. These Snakes have particularly enquiring minds, and they can't pass a museum or book shop without going in to browse. Born researchers, they love to dig and delve into whatever subject has taken their fancy, no matter how obscure. Quite often, they discover something valuable by accident.

Pisces Snake

Pisces Snakes tend to live on their nerves even more than most. These types are friendly up to a point, but they hate disagreements and problems and withdraw when things look unpleasant. They are sexy and sensuous and would much prefer a quiet evening with just one special person than a wild party. In the privacy of their bedroom, anything goes, and Pisces Snakes reveal the naughty side of their characters. No one would guess from the understated elegance of their exteriors what an erotic creature the Pisces Snake really is.

Horse

Aries Horse

Overflowing with energy the Aries Horse just can't sit still for long. These types just have to find an outlet for their phenomenal vitality. They are hardworking, hard-playing, and usually highly popular. Less fun-loving signs might be accused of being workaholics but not the Aries Horse. People born under this sign devote enormous amounts of time to their careers but still have so much spare capacity there is plenty left over for their friends. They always do well in their chosen profession.

Taurus Horse

The Taurus Horse can be a trickier creature. Charming yet logical, he has a very good brain and is not afraid to use it. The only problem is that without warning the Taurus Horse can turn from flighty and fun to immensely stubborn and even an earthquake wouldn't shift him from an entrenched position. Yet treated with understanding and patience, the Taurus Horse can be coaxed to produce wonderful achievements.

Gemini Horse

Gemini types are easily bored, and when they are born in the freedom-loving year of the Horse, this trait tends to be accentuated. Unless their attention is caught and held almost instantly, Gemini Horse subjects kick up their heels and gallop off to find more fun elsewhere. For this reason, they often find it difficult to hold on to a job, and they change careers frequently. Yet once they discover a subject about which they can feel passionate, they employ the whole of their considerable talent and will zoom to the top in record time.

Cancer Horse

The Cancer Horse is a lovable creature with a great many friends. These types tend to lack confidence and need a lot of praise and nurturing, but with the right leadership, they will move mountains. Some signs find them difficult to understand because the Cancer Horse loves to be surrounded by a crowd yet needs a lot of alone time too. Misjudge the mood, and the Cancer Horse can seem bafflingly unfriendly. Yet, stay the course, and these subjects become wonderfully loyal friends.

Leo Horse

People born under the star sign of Leo will be the first to admit they like to show off and when they are also born in the year of the Horse, they enjoy showing off all the more. These types love nothing better than strutting around rocking designer outfits while others look on in admiration. They are not so interested in home decor; it's their own personal appearance which counts most. The Leo Horse would much rather invest time and money boosting their image than shoving their earnings into a bank account to gather dust.

Virgo Horse

Virgo types can be a little solemn and over-devoted to duty, but when they are born in the year of the Horse, they are endowed with a welcome streak of equine frivolity. The Virgo Horse loves to party. He will make sure his work is completed first of course, but once the office door clicks shut behind him, the Virgo Horse really knows how to let his hair down.

Libra Horse

The Libra Horse is another true charmer. Friends and acquaintances by the score fill the address books of these types, and their diaries are crammed with appointments. Honest, trustworthy and helpful, other people can't help gravitating to them. Oddly enough, despite their gregarious nature, these types are also very independent. Sometimes too independent for their own good. They are excellent at giving advice to others but find it almost impossible to take advice themselves.

Scorpio Horse

The Scorpio Horse is a real thrill seeker. These types enjoy life's pleasures, particularly passionate pleasures and go all out to attain them. There is no middle road with the Scorpio Horse. These are all or nothing types. They fling themselves into the project of the moment wholeheartedly or not at all. They tend to see things in black and white and believe others are either for them or against them. In serious moments, the Scorpio Horse subscribes to some surprising conspiracy theories, but mostly they keep these ideas to themselves.

Sagittarius Horse

The star sign of Sagittarius is the sign of the Centaur – half-man half-horse – and when these types are born in the year of the Horse, the equine tendencies are so strong they practically have four hooves. Carefree country-lovers these subjects can't bear to be penned in and never feel totally happy until they are out of doors in some wide-open space. They crave fresh air and regular exercise and do best in joint activities. As long as they can spend enough time out of doors, Sagittarius Horses are blessed with glowing good health.

Capricorn Horse

The Capricorn Horse is a canny beast. These types are great savers. They manage to have fun on a shoestring and stash away every spare penny at the same time. They are prepared to work immensely hard provided the pay is good, and they have a remarkable knack of finding just the right job to make the most of their earning power. The Capricorn Horse likes a good time, and he will never be poor.

Aquarius Horse

When Aquarius meets the Horse, it results in a very curious creature. These types admit to enquiring minds; other less charitable signs might call them nosey parkers. Call them what you may, subjects born under this sign need to know and discover. They often become inventors, and they have a weakness for new gadgets and the latest technology. The Aquarius Horse can be wildly impractical and annoy partners by frittering cash away on their latest obsession. They also tend to fill their living space with peculiar objects from junk shops and car boot sales, which they intend to upcycle into useful treasures. Somehow, they seldom get round to finishing the project.

Pisces Horse

Artistic Pisces adds an unusual dimension to the physical Horse, who normally has little time for cultural frills and foibles. These types are great home entertainers and often gifted cooks as well. They invite a group of friends around at the slightest excuse and can conjure delicious snacks and drinks from the most unpromising larders. They adore company and get melancholy if left alone too long.

Goat

Aries Goat

Normally mild and unassuming, the Goat can become almost argumentative when born under the star sign of Aries. Though friendly and very seldom cross, the Aries Goat will suddenly adopt an unexpectedly stubborn position and stick to it unreasonably even when it's obvious he is wrong. Despite this, these types are blessed with sunny natures and are quickly forgiven. They don't bear a grudge and have no idea – after the awkwardness – that anything unpleasant occurred.

Taurus Goat

Like his Aries cousin, the Taurus Goat can turn stubborn too. These types have a very long fuse. Most people would assume they did not have a temper because it is so rarely displayed. But make them truly angry, and they will explode. Small they may be, but a raging Goat can be a fearful sight. On the other hand, these Goats are more likely to have a sweet tooth than their cousins, so if you do upset them, a choccy treat could work wonders in making amends.

Gemini Goat

The Goat born under Gemini is a terrible worrier. These types seem to use their active minds to dream up all the troubles and problems that could result from every single action. Naturally, this renders decision-making almost impossible. They dither and rethink and ponder until finally someone else makes up their mind for them, at which point they are quite happy. In fact, if the Gemini Goat never had to make another decision, she would be a blissfully content creature.

Cancer Goat

Gentle, soft-hearted and kind, the Cancer Goat is a friend to all in need. These types would give their last penny to a homeless beggar in the street, and they always have a shoulder ready should anyone need to cry on it. Yet they can also be surprisingly moody for what appears to be no reason at all, and this characteristic can be baffling to their friends. No point in wasting time asking what's wrong, they find it difficult to explain. Just wait for the clouds to pass.

Leo Goat

The Leo Goat is a very fine specimen. Warm, friendly and more extrovert than her quieter Goat cousins, she seems to have the confidence other Goats often lack. Look more closely though, and you can find all is not quite as it seems. Frequently, that self-assured appearance is merely a well-presented 'front'. Back in the privacy of their own home, the bold Leo Goat can crumble. In truth, these types are easily hurt.

Virgo Goat

Outwardly vague and preoccupied, the Virgo Goat can turn unexpectedly fussy. These types are easy-going, but they can't stand messy homes, mud in their car or sweet wrappers lying around. Yet they would be genuinely surprised if anyone accused them of being pernickety. They believe they are laid back and good-humoured, which they are. Just don't drop chewing gum on their front path, that's all, and take your shoes off at the door.

Libra Goat

The Libra Goat is obliging to the point of self-sacrifice. These types are truly nice people. Generous with their time as well as their possessions. Unfortunately, their good nature is sometimes exploited by the unscrupulous. The Libra Goat will wear itself out in the service of those in distress, will refuse to hear a bad word about anyone and will remain loyal to friends despite the most intense provocation. The Libra Goat lives to please.

Scorpio Goat

Scorpio Goats are among the most strong-willed of all the Goats. They like to go their own way and hate to have others tell them what to do. They don't mind leaving irksome chores and duties to others, but woe betides anyone who tries to interfere with the Scorpio Goat's pet project. At first sight, they may appear preoccupied and have their heads in the clouds, but beneath that vague exterior, their sharp eyes miss very little. Don't underestimate the Scorpio Goat.

Sagittarius Goat

Sagittarius lends an adventurous streak to the normally cautious Goat make-up, and these types tend to take far more risks than their cousins born at other times of the year. While they still enjoy being taken care of, the Sagittarius Goat prefers cosseting on his return from adventures, not instead of them. These types are often good in business and amaze everyone by doing 'extremely well' apparently by accident.

Capricorn Goat

The Capricorn Goat, in contrast, is a very cautious creature. Danger beckons at every turn and security is top of their list of priorities. This Goat can never get to sleep until every door and window has been locked and secured. Should they find themselves staying in a hotel,

Capricorn Goats will often drag a chair in front of the bedroom door, just in case. These types are difficult to get to know because it takes a while to win their trust, but once they become friends they will be loyal forever and despite their caution – or sensible outlook as they'd call it – they can be very successful.

Aquarius Goat

The Aquarius Goat tends to leap about from one high-minded project to the next. These well-meaning types might be manning a soup kitchen one day and devising a scheme to combat climate change the next. Their grand plans seldom come to fruition because they find the practical details so difficult to put into operation but should they link up with an organisational genius they could achieve great things.

Pisces Goat

The Pisces Goat is a very sensitive soul. These types are often highly gifted, and their best course of action is to find someone to take care of them as soon as possible so that they can get on with cultivating their talents. Left to themselves Pisces Goats will neglect their physical needs, failing to cook proper meals or dress warmly in cold weather. With the right guidance, however, they can work wonders.

Monkey

Aries Monkey

These cheeky types have a charm that is quite irresistible. Energetic and mischievous they adore parties and social gatherings of any kind. They crop up on every guest list because they are so entertaining. The Aries Monkey is a font of funny stories and silly jokes but seldom stands still for long. Friends of the Aries Monkey are often frustrated as their popular companion is so in demand it's difficult to pin her down for a catch-up.

Taurus Monkey

The Monkey born under the star sign of Taurus has a little more weight in his character. These types take life a shade more seriously than their delightfully frivolous cousins. Not that the Taurus Monkey is ever a stick-in-the-mud. It's just that business comes before pleasure with these types, although only just, and the business that catches their eye is not necessarily what others would call business. Taurus Monkey is as captivated by creating a useful container out of an old coffee jar as checking out a balance sheet.

Gemini Monkey

The Gemini Monkey Is a true comedian. Incredibly quick-witted, these types only have to open their mouths, and everyone around them is in stitches. If Oscar Wilde was not a Gemini Monkey, he should have been. People born under this sign could easily make a career in the comedy field if they can be bothered to make enough attempts. Truth is they're just as happy entertaining their friends as a theatre full of people.

Cancer Monkey

These types have a gentler side to their characters. Cancer Monkey's love to tinker with machinery and see how things work. They tend to take things to pieces and then forget to put them together again. They are easily hurt, however, if someone complains about this trait. They genuinely intend to put things right. It is just that somehow they never manage to get round to it, and they never realise that this is a trait they repeat over and over again.

Leo Monkey

The Leo Monkey is a highly adaptable creature. He can be all things to all men while still retaining his own unique personality. Popular, amusing and fond of practical jokes these types are welcome wherever they go. They can sometimes get rather carried away with the sound of their own voices and end up being rather tactless, but such is their charm that everyone forgives them. Occasionally, a practical joke can go too far, but kind-hearted Leo Monkey is horrified if anyone feels hurt, and instantly apologises.

Virgo Monkey

The Virgo Monkey could be a great inventor. The Monkey's natural ingenuity blends with Virgo's patience and fussiness over detail to create a character with the ideas to discover something new and the tenacity to carry on until it is perfected. If they could curb their impulse to rush on to the next brilliant idea when the last is complete, and turned their intention instead to marketing, they could make a fortune.

Libra Monkey

The Monkey born under the sign of Libra is actually a force to be reckoned with though no-one would ever guess it. These types are lovable and fun and have a knack of getting other people to do what they want without even realising they've been talked into it. In fact, Libran Monkeys are first-class manipulators but so skilled at their craft that nobody minds. These types could get away with murder.

Scorpio Monkey

Normally, the Monkey is a real chatterbox, but when Scorpio is added to the mix, you have a primate with the unusual gift of discretion right alongside his natural loquaciousness. These types will happily gossip all day long, but if they need to keep a secret, they are able to do so, to the grave if necessary. Scorpio Monkey could be an actor or a spy – and play each role to perfection. 007 could well have been a Scorpio Monkey.

Sagittarius Monkey

These flexible, amorous, adventure-loving Monkeys add zing to any gathering. These are the guests with the mad-cap ideas who want to jump fully clothed into the swimming pool at midnight and think it terrific fun to see in the New Year on top of Ben Nevis. It's difficult to keep up with the Sagittarius Monkey, but it's certainly fun to try.

Capricorn Monkey

Capricorn Monkeys have their serious side, but they are also flirty types. These are the subjects who charm with ease and tease and joke their conquests into bed. The trouble is Capricorn Monkey often promises more than is deliverable. These types tire more easily than they realise, and can't always put their exciting schemes into action. This rarely stops them trying, of course.

Aquarius Monkey

The Aquarius Monkey is a particularly inventive creature and employs his considerable intellect in trying to discover new ways to save the world. These types often have a hard time in their early years as it takes them decades to realise that not everyone sees the importance of their passions as they do. But, once they understand a different approach is needed, they go on to accomplish much in later life.

Pisces Monkey

The Pisces Monkey can be a puzzling creature. These types are dreamy and amusing one minute and irritable and quick-tempered the next. They can go with the flow so far and then suddenly wonder why no-one can keep up with them when they decide to get a move on. They tend to lack quite so much humour when the joke is on themselves, but most of the time they are agreeable companions.

Rooster

Aries Rooster

Stand well back when confronted with an Aries Rooster. These types are one hundred percent go-getter, and nothing will stand in their way. Aries Rooster can excel at anything to which he puts his mind, and as he frequently puts his mind to business matters, he's likely to end up a billionaire. Think scarlet sports cars, ostentatious homes, and a personal helicopter or two – the owner is bound to be an Aries Rooster.

Taurus Rooster

The Taurus Rooster has a heart of gold but can come over as a bit of a bossy boots, particularly in financial matters. These types believe they have a unique understanding of money and accounts and are forever trying to get more sloppy signs to sharpen up in this department. Even if their manner rankles, it's worth listening to their advice. Annoyingly, they are often right.

Gemini Rooster

The Rooster born under the sign of Gemini would make a terrific private detective were it not for the fact that Roosters find it almost impossible to blend into the background. Gemini Roosters love to find out what's going on and have an uncanny ability to stumble on the one thing you don't wish them to know. They mean no harm, however, and once they find a suitable outlet for their talents, they will go far.

Cancer Rooster

The Rooster born under the sign of Cancer is often a fine-looking creature and knows it. These types are secretly rather vain and behind the scenes take great pains with their appearance. They would die rather than admit it, however, and like to give the impression that their wonderful style is no more than a happy accident. Though they cultivate a relaxed, easy-going manner, a bad hair day or a splash of mud on their new suede boots is enough to send them into a major sulk for hours.

Leo Rooster

Not everyone takes to the Leo Rooster. The Lion is a naturally proud, extrovert sign and when allied to the strutting Rooster, there is a danger of these types ending up as bossy exhibitionists. Yet they really have the kindest of hearts and will leap from their pedestals in an instant to comfort someone who seems upset. A word of warning – they should avoid excessive alcohol as these types can get merry on a sniff of a cider apple.

Virgo Rooster

The Virgo Rooster is a hardworking, dedicated creature, devoted to family, but in an undemonstrative way. Wind this bird up at your peril, however. These types have little sense of humour when it comes to taking a joke, and they will hold a grudge for months if they feel someone has made them look foolish. They hate to be laughed at.

Libra Rooster

The Libra Rooster likes to look good, have a fine home and share his considerable assets with his closest friends. These types enjoy admiration, but they are more subtle than Leo Roosters and don't demand it quite so openly. Libra Rooster is quite happy to give but does expect gratitude in return.

Scorpio Rooster

The Scorpio Rooster is a heroic creature. These types will defend a position to the death. In days of old, many a Scorpio Rooster will have got involved in a duel because these types cannot endure insults, will fight aggression with aggression and will not back down under any circumstances. Foolhardy they may appear, but there is something admirable about them nevertheless.

Sagittarius Rooster

The Sagittarius Rooster tends to be a little excitable and rash. These types are bold and brash and ready for anything. They love to travel and are desperate to see what's over the next hill and around the next bend. Born explorers' they never want to tread the conventional travel path. Let others holiday in Marbella if they wish. Sagittarius Rooster prefers a walking tour of Tibet.

Capricorn Rooster

Capricorn brings a steadying quality to the impulsive Rooster. These types like to achieve, consolidate, and then build again. They believe they are amassing a fortune for their family and they usually do. However, sometimes, their families would prefer a little less security and more attention. Best not to mention it to Capricorn Rooster though – this Rooster is likely to feel hurt and offended.

Aquarius Rooster

The Aquarius Rooster is frequently misunderstood. These types mean well but they tend to be impulsive and speak before they think, accidentally offending others when they do so. In fact, the Aquarius Rooster is a sensitive creature beneath that brash exterior and is easily hurt. If they can learn to count to ten before saying anything controversial, and maybe rephrase, they'd be amazed at how successful they'd become.

Pisces Rooster

The Pisces Rooster has a secret fear. He is terrified that one day he will be terribly poor. These types save hard to stave off that dreadful fate and will only feel totally relaxed when they have a huge nest egg behind them. Despite this, they manage to fall in and out of love regularly and often end up delighting their partners with the wonderful lifestyle they can create.

Dog

Aries Dog

The Aries Dog is a friendly type. Extrovert and sociable these subjects like a lively career and cheerful home life. They are not excessively materialistic, but they tend to make headway in the world without trying too hard. Aries Dog likes to get things done and will bound from one task to the next with energy and enthusiasm.

Taurus Dog

The Dog born under the star sign of Taurus is the most dependable creature in the world. Their word really is their bond, and they will never break a promise while there is breath in their body. They tend to be ultra-conservative with a small 'c'. The men are inclined to be chauvinists, and the women usually hold traditional views. They really do prefer to make their home and family their priority. They are loyal and kind, and people instinctively trust them.

Gemini Dog

The Gemini Dog, in contrast, while never actually dishonest, can be a bit of a sly fox when necessary. The quickest of all Dogs, the Gemini breed gets impatient when the going gets slow and resorts to the odd trick to speed things along. Nevertheless, these types are truthful and honest in their own way and have a knack of falling on their feet... whatever happens.

Cancer Dog

The Cancer Dog was born to be in a settled relationship. These types are never totally happy until they've found their true love and built a cosy home to snuggle up in together. Cancer Dog is not overly concerned with a career. As long as these types earn enough to pay the mortgage and buy life's essentials, they are happy. The right companionship is what they crave. With the perfect partner by their side, they are truly content.

Leo Dog

If Leo Dogs really did have four legs, chances are they would be police dogs. These types are sticklers for law and order. They will not tolerate injustice and will seek out wrongdoers and plague them until they change their ways. Woe betide any workmate who is pilfering pens, making free with office coffee or fiddling expenses. The Leo Dog will force them to own up and make amends. Should you be a victim of injustice, however, Leo Dog will zoom to your aid.

Virgo Dog

The Virgo Dog tends to be a great worrier. A born perfectionist, Virgo Dog agonises over every detail and loses sleep if he suspects he has performed any task badly. These types are very clever and can achieve great things, but too often they fail to enjoy their success because they are too busy worrying they might have made a mistake. The crazy thing is, they very seldom do.

Libra Dog

The Libra Dog believes in 'live and let live'. A laid back, tolerant fellow, Libra Dog likes to lie in the sun and not interfere with anyone. Let sleeping dogs lie is definitely her motto. She will agree to almost anything for a quiet life. Yet it's unwise to push her too far. When there's no alternative, this particular hound can produce a very loud bark.

Scorpio Dog

The Scorpio Dog is as loyal and trustworthy as other canines, but more difficult to get to know. Beneath that amiable exterior is a very suspicious heart. These types don't quite understand why they are so wary of others, but it takes them a long time to learn to trust. Perhaps they are afraid of getting hurt. The idea of marriage fills them with terror, and it takes a very patient partner to get them to the altar. Once married, however, they will be faithful and true.

Sagittarius Dog

The Sagittarius Dog is inexhaustible. These cheerful types are always raring to go and quite happy to join in with any adventure. They love to be part of the gang and are perfectly willing to follow someone else's lead. They don't mind if their ideas are not always accepted; they just like being involved. These types work splendidly in teams and can achieve great things in a group.

Capricorn Dog

The Capricorn Dog is a very caring type. These subjects are happy so long as their loved ones are happy, but they greatly fear that a friend or family member might fall ill. This concern, probably kept secret, gives them real anxiety and should a loved one show worrying symptoms, the Capricorn Dog will suffer sleepless nights until the problem is resolved. When they are not urging their families to keep warm and put on an extra vest, these types are likely to be out and about helping others less fortunate than themselves.

Aquarius Dog

The Aquarius Dog, when young, spends a great deal of time searching for a worthy cause to which they can become devoted. Since there are so many worthy causes from which to choose these types can suffer much heartache as they struggle to pick the right one. When – at last – a niche is found, however, the Aquarius Dog will settle down to a truly contented life of quiet satisfaction. These types need to serve and feel that they are improving life for others. This is their path to happiness.

Pisces Dog

Like the Aquarius breed, the Pisces Dog often has a number of false starts early in life although these are more likely to be of a romantic rather than philanthropic nature. The Pisces Dog wants to find a soulmate but is not averse to exploring a few cul-de-sacs on the way. These types are not promiscuous, however, and when they do find Mr or Miss Right, they are blissfully happy to settle down.

Pig

Aries Pig

The Aries Pig always seems to wear a smile on its face and no wonder. Everything seems to go right for these cheerful types, and they scarcely seem to have to lift a finger to make things fall perfectly into place. In fact, of course, their good luck is the result of sheer hard work, but the Aries Pig has a knack of making work look like play so that nobody realises the effort Pig is putting in.

Taurus Pig

Most Pigs are happy, but the Taurus Pigs really seem quite blissful most of the time. One of their favourite occupations is eating, and they delight in dreaming up sumptuous menus and then creating them for the enjoyment of themselves and their friends. For this reason, Taurus Pigs have a tendency to put on weight. Despite the time they devote to their hobby, however, Taurus Pigs usually do well in their career. Many gifted designers are born under this sign.

Gemini Pig

The Gemini Pig has a brilliant business brain gift-wrapped in a charming, happy go lucky personality. These types usually zoom straight to the top of their chosen tree, but they manage to do so smoothly and easily without ruffling too many feathers on the way. They are popular with their workmates, and later their employees, and nobody can figure out how quite such a nice, down to earth type has ended up in such a position of authority.

Cancer Pig

The Cancer Pig likes to give the impression of being a very hard working type. She is hard working, of course, but perhaps not quite as excessively as she likes others to believe. Secretly, the Cancer Pig makes sure there's plenty of time to spare for fun and indulgence. To the outside world, however, Pig pretends to be constantly slaving away and likes to get regular appreciation for these efforts.

Leo Pig

The Leo Pig is delightful company. Friendly, amusing and very warm and approachable. These types do however have a tremendously lazy streak. Left to themselves, they would not rise till noon, and they prefer someone else to do all the cleaning and cooking. The Leo Pig has to be nagged to make an effort, but when these types do so, they can achieve impressive results.

Virgo Pig

The Virgo Pig, in contrast, is a highly conscientious creature. These types can't abide laziness, and while they are normally kindly, helpful souls who gladly assist others, they will not lift a finger to aid someone who has brought his problems on himself through slovenliness. The Virgo Pig is a clean, contented type who usually achieves a happy life.

Libra Pig

The creative Libra Pig is always dreaming up new ways to improve their home. These types love to be surrounded by beautiful and comfortable things but seldom get round to completing their ideas because they are having such a good time in other ways. This is probably just as well because the minute they decide on one colour scheme, they suddenly see something that might work better. A permanent work in progress is probably the best option.

Scorpio Pig

The Scorpio Pig usually goes far. The amiable Pig boosted by powerful, almost psychic Scorpio can seem turbo-charged at times. These types keep their own counsel more than their chatty cousins, and this often stands them in good stead in business. They can be a little too cautious at times, but they rarely make mistakes.

Sagittarius Pig

Eat, drink and be merry is the motto of the Sagittarius Pig. These types have the intelligence to go far in their careers but, in truth, they would rather party. They love to dress up, get together with a bunch of friends and laugh and dance until dawn. Sagittarius Pig hates to be alone for long, so is always off in search of company.

Capricorn Pig

Pigs are normally broad-minded types, but the Capricorn Pig is a little more staid than his cousins. Nevertheless, being able to narrow their vision gives these types the ability to channel their concentration totally onto the subject in hand, a gift which is vital to success in many professions. For this reason, Capricorn Pigs often make a name for themselves in their chosen career.

Aquarius Pig

Honest, straightforward and popular Aquarius Pigs have more friends than they can count. Always good-humoured and cheerful these types gravitate to those in need and do whatever they can to help. The Aquarius Pig gives copiously to charity and frequently wishes to do more. These types tend to have their heads in the clouds most of the time and for this reason, tend not to give their careers or finances the attention they should. But since worldly success means little to the Aquarius Pig, this hardly matters.

Pisces Pig

The Pisces Pig is a particularly sweet-natured creature. These types are real dreamers. They float around in a world of their own, and people tend to make allowances for them. Yet, from time to time, the Pisces Pig drifts in from his other planet to startle everyone with a stunningly brilliant idea. There is more to the Pisces Pig than meets the eye.

Rat

Aries Rat

Fiery Aries adds more than usual urgency to the sociable Rat. While these types enjoy company, they also tend to be impatient and can get quite bad-tempered and aggressive with anyone who seems to waste their time. Aries Rats do not suffer fools and will stomp off on their own if someone annoys them. In fact, this is the best thing all round. Aries Rats hate to admit it, but they benefit from a little solitude which enables them to calm down and recharge their batteries. Happily, as quickly as these types flare up, they just as quickly cool off again.

Taurus Rat

When Taurus, renowned for a love of luxury and the finer things in life, is born in a comfort-loving Rat year, a true gourmet and bon viveur has entered the world. The Taurus effect enhances the sensuous parts of the Rat personality and lifts them to new heights. Good food is absolutely essential to these types. They don't eat to live; they really do live to eat. Many excellent chefs are born under this sign, and even those folks who don't make catering their career are likely to be outstanding home cooks. Dinner parties thrown by Taurus Rats are memorable affairs. The only drawback with these types is that they can become a little pernickety and overly fussy about details. They also have to watch their weight.

Gemini Rat

While Taurus accentuates the Rat's love of good living, Gemini heightens the Rat's already well-developed social skills. That crowd chuckling and laughing around the witty type in the corner are bound to be listening to a Gemini Rat. Amusing, quick-thinking, and never lost for words, the only things likely to drive Gemini Rats away are bores and undue seriousness. Gemini Rats prefer light, entertaining conversation and head for the hills when things get too heavy. Delightful as they always are however, it is difficult to capture the attention of a Gemini Rat for long. These types love to circulate. They make an entrance and then move on to pastures new. Pinning them down never works. They simply lose interest and with it that famous sparkle.

Cancer Rat

Cancer makes the Rat a little more sensitive and easily hurt than usual. These types are emotional and loving but sometimes come across as martyrs. They work hard but tend to feel, often without good cause, their efforts are not as well appreciated as they should be. Cancer Rats frequently suspect they are being taken for granted at home and at work, but their love of company prevents them from making too big a fuss. Rats are naturally gifted business people, and the Cancer Rat has a particularly good head for financial affairs. These types enjoy working with others, and they are especially well suited to partnerships. However, don't expect the sensitive, feeling Cancer Rat to be a pushover. These types can be surprisingly demanding at work and will not tolerate any laziness on the part of employees.

Leo Rat

Leo Rats usually get to the top. Few people can resist them. The combination of Rat sociability, business acumen and ambition, coupled with extrovert Leo's rather, shall we say, 'pushy', qualities and flair for leadership can't help but power these types to the top of whatever tree they happen to choose to climb. Along the way, however, they may irritate those few less gifted souls who fail to fall under their spell. Such doubters may complain that Leo Rat hogs the limelight and tends to become overbearing at times but since hardly anyone else seems to notice, why should Leo Rat care?

Virgo Rat

As we have already seen, the delightful Rat does have a stingy streak in his make-up, and when the astrological sign of Virgo is added to the mix, this characteristic tends to widen. At best, Virgo Rats are terrific savers and do wonders with their investments. The Rat tendency to squander money on unwise bargains is almost entirely absent in these types, and they often end up seriously rich. At worst, however, in negative types, Virgo Rats can be real Scrooges, grating the last sliver of soap to save on washing powder, sitting in the dark to conserve electricity and attempting their own shoe repairs with stick-on soles, even when they have plenty of money in the bank. Virgo Rats are brilliant at detail; but in negative types, they put this gift to poor use spending far too long on money-saving schemes when they would do much better to look for ways of expanding their income.

Libra Rat

The Libra Rat adores company even more than most. In fact, these types are seldom alone. They have dozens of friends, their phones never stop ringing, and most evenings the Libra Rat is entertaining. Libra Rat enjoys civilised gatherings rather than wild parties and friends will be treated to beautiful music, exquisite food and a supremely comfortable home. These types really can charm the birds off the trees, not with the brilliant repartee of the Gemini Rat but with a warmth and low key humour all their own. These types do tend to be a touch lazier than the usual Rat and their weakness for bargains, particularly in the areas of art and fashion, is more pronounced, but their charm is so strong that partners forgive them for overspending.

Scorpio Rat

It's often said that Rats would make good journalists or detectives because beneath that expansive surface is a highly observant brain. Well the best of them all would be the Rat born under Scorpio. A veritable Sherlock Holmes of a Rat if you wish to be flattering, or a real nosey parker if you don't. These types are endlessly curious. They want to know everything that's going on, who is doing what with whom where and for how long. They may not have any particular use for the information they gather, but they just can't help gathering it all the same. Scorpio Rats often have psychic powers though they may not be aware of this and these powers aid them in their 'research'. Unlike other Rats, those born under Scorpio prefer their own company and like to work alone. When they manage to combine their curiosity and talent for digging out information, there is almost no limit to what they can achieve with their career

Sagittarius Rat

Traditionally Rats have many friends, but the Sagittarius Rat has the not so welcome distinction of collecting a few enemies along the way as well. The Sagittarius Rat finds this quite extraordinary as he never intends to upset anyone. It's just that these types can be forthright to the point of rudeness and an affable nature can only compensate so far. These types are amicable and warm, but when they speak their minds, some people never forgive them. Despite this tendency, Sagittarius Rats have a knack for accumulating money and plough it back into their business to good effect. They manage to be generous, and a bit mean at the same time, which baffles their friends, but those that have not been offended by Sagittarius Rat's tactless tongue tend to stay loyal forever.

Capricorn Rat

Rats are naturally high achievers, but perhaps the highest achiever of them all is likely to be born under the sign of Capricorn. These types are not loud and brilliant like Leo Rats. They tend to be quietly ambitious. They keep in the background, watching what needs to be done, astutely judging who counts and who does not, and then when they are absolutely sure they are on solid ground, they move in. After such preparation, they are unlikely to make a mistake, but if they do they blame themselves, they are bitterly angry, and they resolve never to repeat their stupidity. Reckless these types are not, but their methods produce good results, and they make steady progress towards their goals.

Aquarius Rat

All Rats are blessed with good brains, but few of them think of themselves as intellectuals. The exceptions are the Rats born under the sign of Aquarius. While being friendly and sociable, the Aquarian Rat also needs time alone to think things through and to study the latest subject that has aroused his interest. Perhaps not so adept at business as most Rats, those born under the sign of Aquarius make up for any deficiency in this department by teeming with good ideas. They are intuitive, very hard working and love to be involved in 'people' projects.

Pisces Rat

Pisces Rats tend to be quieter than their more flamboyant brothers and sisters. They are not drawn to the limelight, and they are not so interested in business as other Rats. In fact, working for other people has little appeal for them, although this is what they often end up doing through want of thinking up a better idea. Should a more enterprising Pisces Rat decide to put his mind to business, however, he will often end up self-employed which suits him extremely well. Having taken the plunge, many a self-employed Pisces Rat surprises himself by doing very well indeed. These types can be amazingly shrewd and intuitive, and once these powers are harnessed to the right career, they progress in leaps and bounds. Pisces Rats tend to do well in spite of themselves.

CHAPTER 17: CREATE A WONDERFUL YEAR

By now, you should have got a pretty good idea of the main influences on your life and personality, according to Chinese astrology. But how is 2022 going to shape up for you? Well, that largely depends on how cleverly you play your hand.

Tiger years are traditionally regarded as lucky. Yet they're full of necessary change and upheaval and the pace is fast. The key point is that – according to Chinese astrology – everything should be in balance. So, after the slower, more cautious energy that permeated last year's Year of the Ox, the world needs this fresh impetus as an antidote to restore the planet's balance. After 12 months of consolidation, it's time to move forward again and strike out anew. In 2022, the emphasis will be on innovation, new ideas, bold ventures and idealistic values.

Some signs will find these conditions more comfortable than others. Zodiac creatures that prefer to keep things as they are – those that tend to err on the side of caution and who like to reflect long and hard before making changes – could find 2022 a little nerve-wracking and might like to plan regular de-stressing activities for the coming year. Energetic, always-on-the-go types, however, will be buzzing with excitement. Yet, whichever group you belong to, as long as you're prepared – and you know what you might be up against – you can develop a strategy to ride those waves like a world-class surfer.

Sit back and rely on good fortune alone, because it's a terrific year for your sign, and you could snatch failure from the jaws of success. Navigate any stormy seas with skill and foresight, if it's not such a sunny year for your sign, and you'll sail on to fulfil your dreams. This is always true *in any year*, but doubly so when the mighty Tiger is in charge. Above all, the Tiger supports courageous action, altruistic gestures, kindly behaviour and originality. So, no matter what zodiac sign you were born under, 'Tiger year energy' will help you... if you help yourself.

The future is not set in stone.

Chinese astrology is used very much like a weather forecast, so that you can check out the likely conditions you'll encounter on your journey and plan your route and equipment accordingly. Some signs might need a parasol and sandals; while others require stout walking boots and rain-gear. Yet, properly prepared, both will end up in a good place at the end of the trip.

Finally, it's said that if you feel another sign has a much better outlook than you this year, you can carry a small symbol of that animal with you (in the form of a piece of jewellery, perhaps, or a tiny charm in your pocket or bag) and their good luck will rub off on you. Does it work? For some, maybe, but there's certainly no harm in trying.

Other Top-Rated Books

Linda Dearsley – *the author of this book* – was Doris Stokes' ghost.

Well, more accurately, she was the ghost-writer for Doris Stokes and worked with her for 10 years to produce 7 books, detailing the great lady's life.

In Voices Everywhere, Linda shines a light on her time working with Doris, right from the very early days when Doris was doing private readings in her Fulham flat, to filling the London Palladium and Barbican night after night, to subsequent fame outside the UK. Throughout all this, Doris Stokes never became anyone other than who she was: a kind, generous, and down-to-earth woman with an extraordinary gift, and a fondness for a nice cup of tea. January 6th, 2020, would have been Doris' 100th birthday.

Following Doris' death, Linda chronicles how cynics tried to torpedo the Stokes legacy with accusations of cheating and dishonesty, but how those closest to Doris never believed she was anything other than genuine.

In turn, as the months and years rolled by, more and more intriguing people crossed Linda's path, each with their own unexplainable power, and Doris never seemed far away. From the palmist who saw pictures in people's hands, to the couple whose marriage was predicted by Doris, and the woman who believes she captures departed spirits on camera – the mysterious world of the paranormal, and Doris Stokes' place within it, continues to unfold.

Karina Collins is an acclaimed Tarot reader who has helped people, from all walks of life, to better understand their lives' journeys.

Now, she is on a mission to help you take control of your life – through the power of Tarot – to better explore and understand your purpose and destiny.

Do you have questions about now and your future? Perhaps about making more money, or whether love is on the horizon, or whether you will become happier? Do you want to steer your life in a direction that brings success, pleasure, and fulfilment? Well, Tarot is a means to help you do exactly that! Used for centuries, it provides a powerful tool for unlocking knowledge, divining the future, and delivering shortcuts to the lives we desire.

In this full-colour book, Karina provides explanations and insights into the full 78-card Tarot deck, how to phrase questions most effectively, real-world sample readings, why seemingly scary cards represent opportunities for growth and triumph, and more.

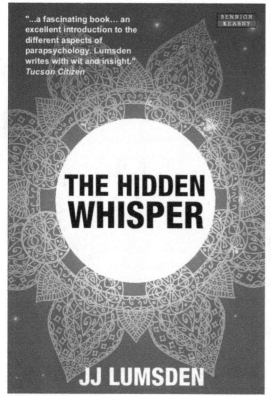

"...a fascinating book... an excellent introduction to the different aspects of parapsychology. Lumsden writes with wit and insight."
Tucson Citizen

BENNION KEARNY

THE HIDDEN WHISPER

JJ LUMSDEN

A paranormal puzzle smoulders in the desert heat of southern Arizona. At the home of Jack and Chloe Monroe, a written message "Leave Now" appears then disappears, a candle in an empty room mysteriously lights itself, and – most enigmatically – an unidentifiable ethereal whisper begins to permeate the house. What was once simply strange now feels sinister. What once seemed a curiosity now seems terrifying.

Dr. Luke Jackson, a British Parapsychologist visiting family nearby, is asked to investigate and quickly finds himself drawn deeper into the series of unexplained events. Time is against him. He has just one week to understand and resolve the poltergeist case before he must depart Arizona.

The Hidden Whisper is the acclaimed paranormal thriller, written by real-life parapsychologist Dr. JJ Lumsden, which offers a rare opportunity to enter the intriguing world of parapsychology through the eyes of Luke Jackson. The fictional narrative is combined with extensive endnotes and references that cover Extra Sensory Perception, Psychokinesis, Haunts, Poltergeists, Out of Body Experiences, and more. If you thought parapsychology was like Ghostbusters – think again…

"This book works on many levels, an excellent introduction to the concepts current in the field of parapsychology… at best you may learn something new, and at worst you'll have read a witty and well-written paranormal detective story" Parascience.

www.BennionKearny.com/paranormal

One of the most common clichés about success – that it is a journey, not a destination – has concealed one of its most defining qualities. Success really is a dynamic and ever-moving process. It is about making the right moves at the right time.

In this absorbing and uplifting book, Jag Shoker – a leading performance coach to business leaders, sports professionals and creative performers – brings the science and inspiration behind success to life. He reveals the 7 Master Moves that combine to create the high performance state that he calls Inspired Movement: the ability to perform an optimal series of moves to create the success you desire most.

The 7 Master Moves of SUCCESS

Jag Shoker

Drawing widely on scientific research, his extensive consultancy experiences, and insights into the successes of top performers in business, sport, and entertainment, 7 Master Moves is a synthesis of the leading-edge thinking, and paradigms, that underpin personal performance and potential.

Building upon key research in fields such as neuroscience, psychology, expert performance and talent development – 7 Master Moves represents an evidence-based 'meta' theory of what really works. Compelling to read, and easy to follow, the book incorporates a strong practical element and shares a number of powerful and practical exercises that can help you apply each Master Move and achieve greater results in your life and work.

Regardless of your profession or passion in life, the 7 Master Moves will reward those who are prepared to work hard to achieve the success that matters most to them.

CPSIA information can be obtained
at www.ICGtesting.com
Printed in the USA
BVHW031803160122
626389BV00011B/281

9 781910 515891